Sustainable Global Happiness

The Journey and the Destination

RANDY A. SILTANEN

Copyright © 2024 Randy Siltanen.

All rights reserved.

ISBN: 979-8-218-35522-7

2026 edition

The ideas presented in this book are general in nature and not intended for use as individualized personal or medical advice. You are advised to consult with your professional healthcare provider in all matters regarding your personal health and well-being.

Cover art: Shutterstock image, by *Unive*.

For Diana

Contents

Prologue 9

Part I: The Journey and the Destination

ONE — The Spinning Coin 15
TWO — The Potential of Stardust 23
THREE — A New Way of Thinking 29

Part II: Preparing for the Journey

FOUR — A Ship Built to Last 39
FIVE — Unfurling the Sails 47

Part III: The Challenges Ahead

SIX — First Things First 57
SEVEN — Core Values 63
EIGHT — Meet Me in the Middle 69
NINE — Bridging our Great Divides 75
TEN — Population Awareness 107
ELEVEN — Rapidly Accelerating Technology 119
TWELVE — The Greater Good 135

Part IV: Good Captains and Good Maps

THIRTEEN — Noble Leadership and Foresight 141
FOURTEEN — A Roadmap to Sustainable Global Happiness 153

Epilogue 161   Acknowledgments 163

"The secret to living well and longer is: eat half, walk double, laugh triple, and love without measure."

-Tibetan proverb

Prologue

THIS LITTLE BOOK can be read over a weekend if you wish – perhaps at a sunny park, or at home with a cup of coffee or tea. In the pages to follow, I offer noble aspirations and guideposts to consider; ideas that aim to improve personal happiness within the greater framework of humankind's collective happiness.

I write as any world citizen, one to another, in the hope that we will celebrate both our differences and similarities, coming together to help achieve the global greater good.

I write to every person on our planet: To young and old people, and rich and poor people; to people of all colors and nations; to agnostics, atheists, and individuals of all religious faiths; to those who call themselves conservative, centrist, or progressive; to peasants and kings; to warriors and pacifists. I write to those who may love me, and to those who may not. Perhaps most of all, I write to my adult children's generation – as the future is indeed theirs to create.

I am not a guru or spiritual counselor. I make no claim to intellectual, religious, or moral authority; and I have no higher connection to God or the cosmos than any other human being. What I am is a father and grandfather; one who wishes for the best that life can bring to his children and their children – and to all citizens of our world, present and future.

I am also a husband, a son, a sibling, and a friend. In many ways, I am probably a lot like you. I have experienced many bright days of great happiness, yet I have also known the deep and dark redoubts of pain and suffering; a fate spared no creature of Earth.

If I possess any unique attribute, it is that of curiosity combined with perseverance – curiosity to read and listen intently, and perseverance to crystalize and synthesize the ideas and works of many talented individuals into a grand world-view; one whose overarching aim is to achieve lasting health and happiness for our Earth and its inhabitants.

The central theme of this book is the ideal of Happiness, which I use as an umbrella term to encompass a wide array of emotions and feelings.

I think that everyone has their own ideas of Happiness. Happiness can be cheerfulness, joy, delight, and exhilaration. Sometimes it is just a quiet inner feeling of fulfillment and satisfaction.

To me, Happiness is also time spent in carefreeness. It is Saturdays. It is standing in a magnificent forest beneath a canopy of ancient sequoia trees. It is swimming in the clear waters of a pristine mountain lake. It is watching a Maui sunset.

For most of us, to be happy also means to possess a sense of dignity. It is knowing that we are cared about, listened to, appreciated, and respected. It is the ability to have some control of our own destiny. It is having families and friends to love, and it is being loved in return.

Happiness is all these things and more. It is all that is good in Life. And if these myriad manifestations of Happiness do indeed share a thread of commonality, it is that of the warm glow of well-being and contentment that comes from a life well-lived. Like most people, I wish for every person on our planet, present and future, to experience these feelings.

But there are prerequisites to Happiness. Similar to Maslow's Hierarchy of Needs, fundamental conditions for Happiness must first be met. These conditions include universal access to clean water, healthy food, safe shelter, and equality of opportunity. And these key foundational layers are themselves supported by the massive twin pillar precepts of social justice and environmental sustainability.

I believe it is our collective responsibility to help fulfill these basic needs for all humanity, providing the foundation from which each person can then pursue their own higher levels of self-actualization and transcendence – and ultimately optimal Happiness.

I believe that perhaps the meaning and purpose of Life are to find and create Happiness; for ourselves, and for *all* present and future inhabitants of a sustainable planet. We can call this notion *Sustainable Global Happiness* – an ideal that is simply a natural manifestation of love: Love for ourselves, love for our neighbors at home and abroad, and love for the gift of Providence that is our magnificent Earth.

The health and happiness of the individual, the collective, and the Earth itself – *Person, People, and Planet* – can be represented by a triangle, as shown at the bottom of this page. Each entity comprises a distinct and equal side of the triangle, and each is an essential and connected component of an integrated whole. What affects one, affects all; today and tomorrow.

This book discusses ideas for finding personal and collective happiness on a safe, just, and flourishing Earth. It also offers insights regarding many present global challenges – notions that aim to help humankind live peacefully and sustainably together on our beautiful planet. Such a feat will require a global citizenry willing to make unceasing efforts at communication, collaboration, and compromise. Each of these actions are critically important, especially in the present climate of cultural division and polarity.

In the lines to follow, I attempt to bring together many of the colors and complexities of Life onto pages of purpose and meaning, hoping to help illuminate pathways to lasting health and happiness for all Earth inhabitants.

The destination of Sustainable Global Happiness is indeed a lofty vision, but it is certainly attainable, and we must relentlessly pursue it.

Never give up!

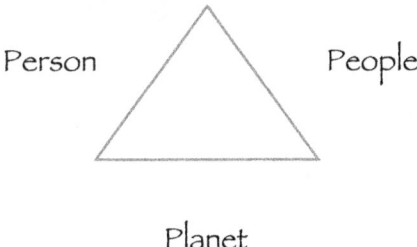

Sustainable Global Happiness is the coming together of Person, People, and Planet to achieve the full potential of each.

Sustainable Global Happiness

PART I

The Journey and The Destination

ONE

The Spinning Coin

IT IS THE last day of Summer. Soon the tamarack trees will change color, and spires of gold will briefly grace the green alpine forest of pine, spruce, and fir.

The path I am on this morning follows a small river near my home, climbing south through many quiet meadows, glens, and forested hillsides of wilderness. My destination is the river headwaters – a spectacular high mountain lake, nestled cozily in a natural amphitheater carved out by glacial erosion.

About a mile or so up the trail, I pass through a small grove of aspen trees beginning to lighten in color. From here, a picturesque lake can be seen back in the distance – an elongated blue sapphire set before the tawny grasses of the prairie beyond. A soft breeze interrupts the stillness. Each leaf of a nearby quaking aspen trembles in unique cadence, creating the overall shimmering effect that gives this tree its name.

In about a month, the tamarack needles and aspen leaves will descend to the ground, and barren branches will be covered by snow. Fresh new foliage will appear again next spring, but that seems a long time from now. I take another look back, and then continue up the trail.

The changing forest is a reminder of the impermanence of Life and Nature. A part of me wishes to cling to this present moment; this brief instant of existence. It is tempting to long for Life to be safe, secure, and permanent. I can imagine an interruption of time itself, in a place where nothing ever changes – where bright green leaves forever flutter in a summer breeze, and my family and friends are always in my life.

Struggling with the inevitability of change, it is easy to share the pain of poet Dylan Thomas, as he begs his passing father to "rage, rage against the dying of the light." At times, Life can seem to exist upon a fragile precipice, perched perilously over death. I sometimes think one of my own loved ones could be taken from me all too quickly, slipping off into the night.

Further up the trail, a sunlit peak can be seen in the distance. I enter a heavily-forested region, nearly impenetrable to the Sun. Fallen tree limbs litter the surrounding forest floor. Here, darkness permeates between and beyond tall firs; weathered sentinels standing guard before the woodland depths.

I sometimes experience a sense of apprehension when walking in dense timber stands like this, where distant vision is constrained. Nature is simultaneously beautiful and terrifying. I imagine a cougar lurking in the shadows, tracking my movements along the trail. I have seen them before in these mountains. I find a stout stick to carry, and walk a little faster.

It is interesting how thoughts float randomly along the streams of our human consciousness – somewhat like leaves drifting down a mountain brook. As filtered reflections of our experiential lives, some thoughts are pleasant, and some are not – and we often have little control over what the current will bring. If we wish to do so, we can choose to engage with a thought; much like reaching for a passing leaf in the water to examine more closely. Or, if we prefer, we can simply pay no heed to these fleeting contemplations, letting them disappear downstream beyond the bend.

Just up the path, sunbeams once again emerge between tree branches, casting beautiful patterns of dappled light upon the forest floor. In places like this, where brightness conquers darkness, lighter thoughts present themselves more abundantly. I feel brave again.

Nearly one hundred years ago, Khalil Gibron wrote that our children are not truly ours; rather they are the sons and daughters of Life's longing for itself. He said that our children do indeed come through us, but they are not from us.

And regarding our lovers, Gibron said that there must be spaces in our togetherness: Stand together; yet not too near together. He said to remember that the oak tree and the cypress grow not in each other's shadow – there must be space for the winds of the heavens to dance between them.

Perhaps everything we cherish, and every person we love, must be surrendered to Providence – the divine guardianship of God or Nature. Like seeds scattered by the wind, forces beyond our control will send everything and everyone tumbling where they will.

Although it is difficult to accept impermanence, we cannot tether ourselves to the ephemeral. A hawk does not plummet through the air, attempting to arrest its freefall by hopelessly clutching at clouds. It stays aloft by merely opening its wings to the prevailing currents – *relinquishing* control, to *gain* control.

Our families and friends come and go, like clouds in an overhead sky. Our loved ones, too, change in size and shape; moving from here to there, sharing their tears of sorrow and joy. And sometimes, if we are lucky, they offer to us their love and friendship – exquisite rainbows emerging through the pain and promise of a million raindrops. We must cherish our time shared together; as our Earthly lives will someday, too, vanish like the clouds.

Life on our planet is a story of constant change, existing within a universe that evolves via unceasing creative destruction. Here, dying is an essential part of living, and sadness is an ever-present counterbalance to happiness.

What should we make of this fragile existence, this fleeting moment in time? Do we possess the courage to surrender ourselves to the relentless vicissitudes of Life, trusting the winds of Providence to keep us aloft? Is it possible to not merely resign ourselves to this existence, but to gladly accept the parts we cannot change?

A part of our individual life is certainly under our control. We are a human being – but a human being *what*? What exactly are we *being*? Are we being an optimistic person and a positive force for good? On Earth, no one ever makes it out of here alive. Whether a person chooses to be happy, angry, or sad, the human story always ends the same – in a final chapter where we, the protagonist, must always perish. Will our life have made a difference?

Our universe is made up of a fantastic array of cycles in constant flux; countless intricate systems of complexities nested within systems of ever-greater complexities. These cycles balance each other, and all continuously evolve together.

Our very lives are deeply interwoven into this elaborate web, each with our own roiling milieus of exquisitely integrated systems, all steeped in a tenuous equilibrium of opposing forces.

In this extraordinary Life, hope coexists with fear, good with evil, and happiness with sadness. Here, heaven is other people – and hell is other people. There are two sides to every spinning coin, and each side is as real and true as the other. Is it heads, or is it tails?

It is both.

This paradoxical presence of contemporaneous contradictions has the potential to create a state of unease. We humans often seem to favor a mindset of absolutism much more than the experience of conflicting ideas.

We generally do not like uncertainty, preferring exact answers instead of "either or both" scenarios. Maybe it uses less energy for us to think this way. Or perhaps the ability to mentally categorize experiences precisely one way or the other confers a genetic advantage. For an early hunter-gatherer, a lack of decisiveness and certainty – at least in emergent situations – may have led to poor outcomes.

In any event, we can choose to observe Life as we wish. And, similar to Schrodinger's quantum-state theory of physics, it is the very act of observation itself that determines our unique experience.

Humans possess the ability to focus on what we wish – and we can thus shape our own reality.

Life is awful – and life is wonderful. It is simultaneously heaven and hell; sadness and happiness; heads and tails. Nevertheless, it is within our power to momentarily interrupt the spinning of the coin, and view the side we favor.

We see what we look for. And what we see, we often become. Look for darkness, and we will find it. Look for light, and that will surely be ours as well.

We can therefore choose to look for Happiness – and try to create Happiness for others, too. We can choose to consider the idea of death as an emergence into light, rather than fading into darkness.

We can decide to think of Life as a wonderful novel, filled mostly with long, lyrical sentences of triumph and happiness – even if sometimes punctuated by episodes of tragedy and grief. The commas, semi-colons, and periods can be extraordinarily painful interludes, to be sure. However, they may perhaps also act to highlight and add to the narrative, helping to bring perspective and meaning to the various passages of our lives.

We can choose to find something to smile and laugh about every day; if only for a moment in times of challenge. We can decide to think positively about all aspects of humankind's existence, remaining forever astonished and grateful for the marvelously interconnected beauty of Life in our universe – despite its apparent unfairness.

…And, we can choose to think that our universe, with all its joys and sorrows, is perhaps as good as one can possibly be.

About a mile or so beyond the halfway point to the lake, the relatively steep grade of the trail becomes a gentle rise, and the vista more expansive. Up here the river is but a small stream, having yet to reach its full potential. Murmuring in hushed cathedral tones, its waters meander leisurely through an amber grassy meadow, as if to savor this very peaceful part of its journey. Diana and I once stopped and sat along a bend here, dipping our feet into the cool waters beside the bank as we enjoyed our lunch.

After walking another mile or two, I approach the east shore of my destination. Beyond the glistening lake, a burnt-red cape of brushy foliage majestically drapes the slopes of the adjacent mountainside. To the southwest lies a high basin, above which is a rugged crest smartly capped by an early first snow. It is a spectacular scene.

Sometimes while at a high mountain lake like this, especially if a person is alone, it can seem that a presence from some place beyond is creating a dialogue of sorts. If you happen to be located at a proper position relative to the overhead Sun, rays of light will reflect off small water ripples and into your field of vision. And then, if a passing breeze blows favorably, it may send a thousand glittering diamonds skittering across the surface, right toward you – a fleeting gift of beauty to consider and remember.

Soon it is mid-afternoon, and time to go back home. The trail to the high lake follows an up and back route, and I look forward to experiencing the sights and sounds along the path once again. I begin the return trip to the trailhead, allowing enough time to unhurriedly enjoy the mountain environment before sunset.

On the way back, I explore a small tributary of the river, flowing down from another nearby lake. The tiny creek's presence is announced by a soft gurgling melody, beckoning me to come to the places where water falls upon water. Only a few feet wide, and just deep enough to hold a few small brook trout, the stream is partly hidden from view by tall grasses and brush. I follow the gentle sounds of the water, welcoming new discoveries beyond each turn. It is a privilege to experience such intimate invitations as these; into the serene and secret rooms of Nature.

I return to the trail and walk a bit further, stopping to sit at the place where Diana and I had eaten lunch two years prior. Here, when the light is perfect, afternoon sunrays reflect brightly off the meadow stream, creating a winding strand of silver to adorn the mountain landscape. The wildflowers have already surrendered their blooms for the season, but colorful grasses and deciduous foliage further decorate the scene.

Across the stream, a pair of Clark's Nutcracker birds are perched high upon adjacent pine trees. They are aware of my presence, but appear more interested in the surrounding meadow ecosystem.

Resting on the stream bank, I examine the small terminal seeds of a blade of wild grass. I consider their place against the immensity of the surrounding mountains below a vibrant blue sky. I will visit them again next year, when they have become wild grasses of their own.

In these mountains my thoughts turn to my family and friends, to my trials and tribulations, to my accomplishments and failures. I marvel at how they intermix with the timeless dreams and desires of countless other human hearts – past, present and future – and with the infinity of other Earth organisms and ecosystems, each an integral part of this incredible journey of our planet.

I take a last look at the meadow scene. The Sun has fallen closer to the western peaks. It is time to get moving. It will take a couple of hours to get back to the trailhead.

Back to the very place I started.

TWO
The Potential of Stardust

OVER FIVE BILLION years ago, in the Orion arm of our Milky Way galaxy, a number of massive stars exploded as supernovas into the darkness. Evidence suggests that our planet's chemical elements were thus born into existence – blasted bits of matter forged in a series of chain reactions, fueled by the intense heat of crucibles of stunning creativity.

Over time, the resultant immense cloud of cosmic dust underwent a gravitational collapse into numerous smaller systems, each containing a central star.

Our own solar system is thought to have been created this way; scattered elements traveling through space, bumping into each other, eventually coalescing into larger and larger structures. Over millions of years, through accretion, stellar dust became the planets that now orbit our Sun – including our own planet Earth.

Humankind journeys upon a magnificent planet built of stardust; one whose story began in the fiery heat of exploding stars. We are each but one of eight billion human beings existing here, each a living extension of our planet – stardust living on stardust.

Sharing a common genesis, every creature and object of our planet is configured from the same pool of atomic and sub-atomic particles, once discharged into space in tremendous stellar blasts. The air in our lungs, the minerals in our bones, and the water in our tissues are not ours alone – as our bodies continuously borrow and return from a giant repository of recyclable eternal elementary building blocks. We share these particles with the atmosphere and oceans, with mountain tops and valley floors, and with all other creatures, great and small.

Each of our atoms possess an eternal energy; an energy present since the beginning of the universe; an energy that is continuously repurposed, but never destroyed.

Somehow, miraculously, the energies of coalesced elementary particles and atoms became harnessed into the indescribable force that is the spark of Life – a force that continues to manifest itself in gloriously extraordinary variations. From simple lichen on glacial rocks, to butterflies and lions, and even to highly conscious beings like you and me, each creature of Earth embraces its own unique configuration of stardust, and its own version of living.

Human beings are lucky. Endowed with an evolving consciousness, we have the exceptional ability to fully experience life in all its grandeur. Consciousness allows us to love and to be loved. It offers an awareness of beauty, in all its forms. It even gives us the ability to think about our own thoughts.

Consciousness has also bestowed upon humankind the remarkable capacity to help forge its own destiny. This is a wonderful gift indeed – however, it is also one that comes with the tremendous responsibility of stewardship of our planet and all its citizens and creatures, present *and* future. How will we collectively choose to honor this great duty?

Together, at our best, we are a magnificent species. Over the course of our existence, we have created amazing civilizations, beautiful works of art, and music that touches the heart. We have written profound books that offer fascinating philosophies of life. We have scaled tall mountains and traversed deep seas. We have even learned how to retrieve minerals from the depths of our planet; combining and reshaping them to build rocket ships that can return these elements back to the stars from which they came. The extraordinary potential of stardust, *our* potential, is nearly limitless.

Who could imagine such a thing?

Our Human Condition

Humankind's potential is truly astounding. Yet, even with such incredible human *potential*, our human *condition* still suffers. Indeed, individual self-interests often work as gravitational counterforces to the shared ascension of humanity.

The journey ahead offers great promise, but also the possibility of great peril. Individually and collectively, we have the potential to flourish or to fail; depending on the paths we take, and how we choose to support one another and our planet.

The individual, the collective, and the Earth itself – *Person, People, and Planet* – are inseparably connected; each entity an equal component of a greater whole. Personal happiness is best achieved within a global context, as focusing exclusively on *Person* diminishes both *People* and *Planet*. Each of our actions, good or bad, have an effect on everything else; eventually coming back to us, influencing our own personal wellness.

Part of humanity's predilection for self-focus comes naturally. The effects of nature and nurture often incline humans to value self over tribe, and one's individual tribe over all others. We also tend to elevate issues of today over those of tomorrow.

When our ancient hunter-gatherer ancestors demonstrated certain characteristics – such as balancing a degree of self-focus with compassion, cooperation, and loyalty toward other tribal members – they flourished within their factions. They were therefore more likely to live long enough to pass their genes on to people like you and me. Likewise, members of tribes that outcompeted neighboring groups were more likely to survive than those that did not.

Today, much of our way of thinking is based on individual and tribal survival strategies that were naturally-selected over thousands of generations. The lives and stories of countless ancestors are imbedded in our cellular DNA; creating a somewhat immutable blueprint that partly fashions our subconscious thoughts and actions.

But, of course, we human beings are not mere slaves to our chromosomes. Although our foundational thought processes are partly derived from an individualized genetic playbook, they are further forged by the heat and hammers of cultural influence – the evolving customs and spiritual beliefs wrought by our social environment.

Individual value systems are created by both nature and nurture; *nature* coming from our genes, and *nurture* from our friends, teachers, families, and faith communities – as well as from our televisions, laptop computers, and smartphones. We often become what we see and what we hear.

…But it does not end there. Our human value-systems and thought processes can continue to evolve even more, *beyond* nature and nurture. This happens when we choose to further develop our sense of *awareness;* reaching above the subconscious constraints of DNA and cultural influences, challenging ourselves to *consciously* think differently.

Of Two Minds

Humans are evolving composites of a volitional consciousness inseparably connected to a subconscious being. It is as if our conscious thoughts ride within the wild creature that is our subconscious mind and body. The subconscious part of us **feels and reacts** quickly; whereas our conscious mind **thinks and responds** in a slower, more deliberate fashion. These conscious and subconscious entities remain intimately entwined with each other; a fluidic coupling engaged in an elaborate dance of ever-changing acquiescence and dominance.

There are certainly times when our conscious mind must surrender some control to our subconscious self. When throwing a baseball, a pitcher must simply visualize throwing a strike; *letting* it happen, rather than trying to *make* it happen with too much conscious thought.

Nevertheless, taming the subconscious self is sometimes necessary in today's world. Indeed, this has been an essential factor in the ascension of humankind. Left alone, our subconscious mind is often concerned more with self and immediacy; and much less about the fate of others and the future.

In 1951, Argentine President Juan Peron famously said: "The masses don't think, the masses feel."

Throughout the world, and across the political spectrum, many leaders and media commentators today still attempt to appeal to humankind's primitive subconscious *feelings* of fear and greed, rather than to our more advanced *cognitive* sensibilities. We must be cautious of those who deliver divisive diatribes; often paradoxically peppered with attempts at humor, religiosity, or patriotism.

We must remain acutely aware of the human propensity to be mesmerized by carefully-crafted tales offering overly simple solutions to very complex problems; stories that sometimes insidiously beckon us to silence the better angels of our nature.

We must be wary of hypnotizing speeches that implore us to doff the hard-won cloak of humankind's evolving civility; words that stoke emotions of intense tribalism, and sometimes even suggest violence as an appropriate means to an end.

We must also question the proclamations of global citizens, at home and abroad, who believe that their nation should always come first – yet carry holy books that declare such things as "The last will be first, and the first will be last," and "Love your neighbor as yourself."

Individually and collectively, we can create a grand narrative for humankind. We can seek out leaders who offer positive messages of peace, hope, and concern for others. We can walk with fellow citizens who champion noble aspirations of national and global unity, justice for all world inhabitants, and great care of our Earth.

It is perhaps the very nature of our subconscious mind and body to survive; to elevate self and immediacy over concern for others and the future. However, what once worked for small tribes of ancient hunter-gatherers does not always work so well for us today. The various civilizations of Earth are now all interconnected, each just a small sub-group of one massive tribe of humanity.

Our world is changing rapidly, and evolutionary processes must keep pace with the needs of a global populace of 8 billion people. We cannot afford to simply *feel and react* – putting self before country, and country before planet. The universal rule is the same for every creature and civilization on Earth: Evolve or perish.

Today, we must consciously **think and respond** more than ever before; working together globally to plan a common future of health and happiness for one and all. And, to best do so, we must begin to think differently…

We must learn to see to see the world anew.

THREE

A New Way of Thinking

AWARENESS IS A manifestation of a higher level of evolving consciousness, bestowing upon humans the near magical capacity to cognitively be in two places at once. Fully engaged up-close in the present moment, we can also simultaneously observe Life from a distance.

Awareness has been described as similar to being drenched in a passing rainstorm, while at the same time viewing it from afar – and perhaps noting it is just one of many storms.

Self-awareness is the ability to see our own lives from a distance. It allows us to determine if our current actions are indeed congruent with our personal values and life goals. It lets us know if we are acting in the interest of the few or of the many, and whether we are elevating our current concerns over those of countless future generations.

To be optimally self-aware means to possess the ability to impartially judge our own actions from afar. It means to be firm but fair with ourselves – just like we would try to be with someone else.

"The unexamined life is not a life worth living."
-Socrates

Some people often give themselves a free pass far too generously, seeing their own actions through rose-colored glasses. Others reside on the opposite end of the spectrum; demanding self-perfection, and constantly berating themselves for not being faultless.

Like everything else in Life, optimal self-examination is a delicate balancing act, where a tenuous point of equilibrium usually resides near the middle. We must acknowledge our faults, yet we must also judge ourselves more by our intentions and efforts, and less by our results.

Each morning when we awaken, we can meditate on a few personal characteristics to improve upon, and then balance this by considering some positive traits that we may also often demonstrate. It is essential to live a life of love for others – and to always love ourselves as well.

Immersed in the complexities of daily living, it can be difficult to break away from our sequestered everyday lives; to become more *aware*. We may dream of vacating the chrysalis of self and immediacy, rising high on wings of transcendent thought – but right now we may need to prepare dinner, finish that project at work or school, or drive our kids to their soccer games.

Cultivating self-awareness can be even more difficult for citizens in economically-developing countries, where many people may have even less time and resources to indulge in contemplative thought.

Yet, despite these constraints, it is imperative that humankind frequently pauses to reflect upon itself. We must be sure that we are headed in the right direction – personally and collectively. We must stand back and metaphorically view ourselves and Life from a distant vantage point, impartially examining our motives and our present course of action.

"We must learn to see life anew."
-Albert Einstein

From this place of higher thought, we can behold the absolute magnificence of our universe. Here, we can observe the journey of our Earth in its totality. We can also more clearly see humanity's place on this planet – and our own individual place within humanity.

Immersed in this panoramic perspective, we can experience a profound awareness of the events of today – framed between a knowledge of yesterday and a vision of tomorrow. Past, present, and future, seen together as one.

From here, we can visualize the ascending curve of humankind's potential destiny. We can see our chosen destination in the distance – a forever of health and happiness for our Earth and all its inhabitants. And we know that we must always keep this vision squarely in our sight.

From this place of higher consciousness, we can see that time and distance are relative. We note that humankind exists in a very small sliver of time, lived out on a relatively tiny speck of dust, suspended in an impossibly vast and nearly timeless universe.

We can observe that time itself is somewhat of an illusion, and that distance is markedly influenced by perception. We can see that a small child dying across the globe one hundred years from now – due to violence, hunger, or treatable disease – is really not that different than if she perishes right here in our arms today.

We can see that we are all in this together; that our brother's victory is our victory, that our planet's success is our success, and that the past, present, and future are inseparably connected.

Shaping Destiny

Humankind can never completely hold back the inexorable forces of destiny. These powerful forces are partly predetermined by immutable laws of Nature. Ocean tides will continue to rise and fall with the phases of our Moon; our Earth will revolve exactly one time around its axis every twenty-four hours; and clusters of galaxies of our universe are perhaps fated to forever expand outward from their point of common origin.

The destiny of human beings is also in part predetermined. We will all experience days of joy and sorrow – and of triumph and loss – no matter what we wish, or what actions we take. We will all witness or experience wars; and celebrations of peace, too. Eventually, our earthly lives will come to an end.

But not everything in our universe is predetermined. Although it is not possible to absolutely control the course of Earth's journey, we can certainly nudge the trajectory a bit. In many ways we can alter the course of our own evolution.

Humankind can choose to live either at war or in peace with itself. We have the capacity to alter the temperature of our Earth and its atmosphere, and to partly control the rise or fall of the waters of our oceans. We have the power to either save or destroy many of our planet's remarkably beautiful creatures and complex ecosystems. We can thus change the course of our own destiny, for ill or good.

We are all in this together; every single one of us. The fate of each individual person is inextricably entwined with that of the collective, and of the Earth itself.

Like Sisyphus shouldering his great boulder, our collective charge is to push our destiny ever-upward. We cannot accomplish this grand commission individually, or even as just one nation.

It is imperative that *all* humanity comes together in a unified group effort, much like the linked behavior of other species in Nature—as evidenced by flocks of migratory birds, colonies of bees and ants, and the beautifully synchronized movements of schools of fish. It is crucially important that we understand our mutual interdependence with each other, as well as with our Earth and all its ecosystems and creatures – knowing that altering the evolution of one, will certainly alter the evolution of all.

To what grand destiny shall we guide such interconnected and extraordinary potential? Where shall we go?...

It is imperative that humankind resolutely determines our shared ultimate destination – and that we also create a plan of action to get there. This vision must be inspired by a new way of seeing the world; a new *transcendent* way of thinking.

Transcendence is the ability to rise through; to attain greater awareness; to give of oneself to something greater than oneself. It means knowing that optimal *individual* happiness is interwoven within the greater fabric of collective *global* happiness. It means to love deeply, and to love broadly.

Transcendent thought allows us to create a vision of a safe, just, and flourishing Earth.

Sustainable Global Happiness

Presently, humankind appears to be somewhat lost. Perhaps this is because we don't really know where we want to go. Aimlessly adrift, our eyes seem focused mostly on ourselves and our own small crew.

If we are to find our way, it is imperative that we look past the bow – beyond ourselves and beyond today – coming together in search of a common destination.

The American astronomer Carl Sagan said:

> "If we crave some cosmic purpose,
> then let us find ourselves a worthy goal."

Perhaps it is all really quite simple. Maybe the *meaning* of Life is Happiness, and the *purpose* of Life is to find, create and share Happiness. This precept holds that each person must endeavor to find and create happiness for themselves – *and* for all present and future inhabitants of a sustainable planet.

This overarching ideal can be expressed in just three words: **Sustainable Global Happiness**. This notion can serve as humanity's "worthy goal," the desired ultimate destination of every person, city, state, province, and nation.

Each word is uniquely important: **Happiness**, because happiness could quite possibly be the meaning and purpose of life; **Global** Happiness, because individual happiness is inseparably connected with the happiness of all world citizens; and **Sustainable** Global Happiness, because a sustainable and regenerative Earth is an absolute prerequisite for humanity's present and future existence.

There is only one us, one planet that is home to one global body of Life. Each individual creature is a unique manifestation of the inventiveness of a common beginning, and each is an essential interwoven part of a greater Earth and universe ecosystem.

On this planet, everyone and everything are connected. If we hurt but one part, we hurt the whole. And when we improve but one part, we improve the whole. This is the premise, and the promise, of the words on these pages.

The journey to Sustainable Global Happiness is illuminated by a brilliant guiding light: The transcendent idea that the individual, the collective, and the Earth itself – *Person, People, and Planet* – are equal and inseparable, in time and in space.

This idea requires an expansion of awareness, spatially and temporally; from inner self, to outer other; from me today, to you tomorrow.

The journey to Sustainable Global Happiness acknowledges our human condition, while demonstrating a resolute belief in humanity's extraordinary potential.

"Some men see things as they are, and ask why. I dream of things that never were and ask why not."
-Robert F. Kennedy

It is quite likely there are people who will consider the ideal of Sustainable Global Happiness to be an unattainable utopian dream – which is perhaps fair enough. It is true that humankind cannot create an absolutely perfect world, as human beings will likely always be flawed. But it is very possible to come *close* to our noble and lofty aspirations – certainly a lot closer than we are today. Happiness does not require absolute perfection.

If a person chooses to dismiss the notion of Sustainable Global Happiness as a naive or unattainable goal, it is fair to ask that they offer a more compelling narrative of their own. They must present a superior guiding principle, a better recommended path forward, and a nobler ultimate desired destination.

If we believe it is our prime directive to love and honor God, how better to manifest this than to help create health and happiness for our planet and all its inhabitants, present and future?

The status quo is surely not working as well as possible. Nothing changes if nothing changes. We must dream big.

When striving for a better today and tomorrow, it is essential to keep the ultimate goal of Sustainable Global Happiness at the forefront of our collective consciousness. Every vote cast, and every law passed, should be made with this destination in mind.

Built on the granite principle of achieving lasting greater good, the goal of Sustainable Global Happiness is an unassailable promontory; forever holding firm against the storms of non-benevolence. It is an ideal that binds humankind together; across oceans and continents, across religion and culture, across skin color, gender, sexual orientation, political affiliation, age, and all our other many differences.

Journeying together toward our common destination, we can create lasting health and happiness for ourselves, for our neighbors, and for our Earth – today and every day.

It seems there is a commonality between humankind's quest for Happiness, and Earth's unending trek around its bright star. Each year, our planet ends its orbit where it first began, only to unceasingly continue its journey into another year – going nowhere, yet going everywhere.

Likewise, it can seem that there really is no finish line to Happiness. Individually and collectively, a new goal or challenge appears to remain forever in front of us. We may imagine we will someday reach our destination of Happiness – maybe after we finish college…or find a life companion…or buy a new home…or retire from our job.

But maybe it is in the journey itself, the daily challenges and small victories within the trek, in which the destination of Happiness is truly found.

If we were to build a ship and sail around the world, we would ultimately end up in the same waters from which we started. Our great quest would indeed be accomplished – but the true adventure would come from the seas, landscapes, cultures, and weather encountered along the way.

It is certainly important to make plans for a future of Sustainable Global Happiness, but it is likewise essential to find and create Happiness in the present moment as well. Happiness is all around us, right here and right now. We see what we look for.

In many ways, the Journey *is* the Destination.

PART II

Preparing for the Journey

FOUR
A Ship Built to Last

TO BE AN effective force for global health and Happiness, it is imperative that we each optimize our personal well-being; maximizing our physical and mental health. *Personal* wellness is an integral part of *global* wellness, and both body and mind must be as strong and resilient as possible.

This chapter suggests various health strategies to consider; ideas that can enhance the physical health and longevity of our personal body – helping build a ship sturdy enough to withstand the storms of a nearly one-hundred-year journey. In the chapter to follow, ideas will then be offered that can help create a powerful mind – unfurling our sails to harness the winds of knowledge, imagination, and character.

A robust body and mind together provide humans the capacity to help create sustainable health and happiness for our planet and all its inhabitants. In a virtuous cycle, our efforts come back to us, touching our own lives, increasing our own personal wellness.

To build and maintain a strong body, we must energize ourselves with nutrient-rich foods and restful sleep. We can then use some of this energy to increase our physical strength, endurance, and resilience.

It starts with a diet that is good for us – and good for our planet.

Eat Locally-Produced Organic Whole Foods

The core idea of a healthy and sustainable nutrition plan is to eat a wide variety of predominantly locally-produced organic whole foods, favoring mostly plants and plant-based products.

A healthy meal could start with generous portions of vegetables and fruits showcased on the front half of the plate. About one-fourth of the plate could hold foods made from unprocessed whole grains – such as wheat, oats, corn, or rice. The remaining one-fourth of the plate could feature healthy protein sources – such as tree nuts and legumes, or ethically-sourced seafood, meat, dairy, or eggs.

The Harvard Healthy Eating Plate can serve as good dietary outline – and it can be made even better by choosing *organic* food options.

To optimize personal and planetary health, protein choices can favor plant-based sources (e.g., beans, peas, lentils, chickpeas, nuts) – healthy options that are Earth-and-body-friendly. If one chooses to eat beef, it is optimally obtained from local free-range, grass-fed and grass-finished animals, and used in moderation due to environmental considerations. If pork is consumed, local products from animals raised cage-free in a pasture can be selected. Poultry products and eggs are also ideally obtained from free-range and cage-free animals.

Seafood is often best consumed wild; however, regarding human health and environmental concerns, certain farmed species can also be a good choice. The Monterey Bay Aquarium Seafood Watch website provides in-depth species-specific recommendations in this regard. A Marine Stewardship Council seafood package label can verify that wild-caught food items were obtained from a sustainable source.

Another essential element of an Earth-and-body-friendly diet is to choose **organically-grown** food. This practice helps keep dangerous pesticide residues from entering our bodies, and also helps preserve our planet for all present and future generations – a win-win strategy.

It is important to read the label on every packaged food product that is purchased; choosing items that are low-sodium and low-sugar, and those that contain no additives, unnatural dyes, or preservatives. If we are unfamiliar with the name of an ingredient on a label, it may not be good for us. As much as possible, it is important to favor whole, non-processed foods that do not come in a box, jar, or wrapper.

In a healthy diet, the vast majority of fluid intake should be clean filtered water – and *not* stored in plastic bottles (due to personal and planetary health concerns). Blended fruit and veggie smoothies consumed in moderation are generally healthful, but filtered fruit juices and sodas should be mostly avoided. To optimize health and longevity, it is also advisable to generally abstain from alcoholic beverages.

Foods containing *added* sugars are best consumed only as a rare treat. Excessive sugar intake can lead to abnormal insulin responses; and has been correlated with inflammation, diabetes, obesity, heart disease, stroke, cancer, neuropsychiatric disease, and dementia.

Cravings for sweets can be healthfully satisfied by eating fruit. Although fruits do indeed contain sugars, they are also filled with beneficial substances called *phytonutrients*. In addition, fruits contain lots of fiber. Fiber slows sugar absorption; thereby helping to dampen blood sugar and insulin spikes that can damage our bodies. Eating fruit alongside a serving of healthy proteins and fats (such as a handful of non-salted nuts) can also further help smooth out blood sugar levels.

Eating **locally-produced** food encourages biodiversity, while also supporting regional economies. It also significantly reduces fuel usage, greenhouse gas emissions, and other pollution. Recall, too, that food can lose flavor and nutritional value during long-distance transport.

One way to remember this plan for healthy eating is to use the acronym **FLOW**, especially when shopping for food. The **FLOW** diet emphasizes **F**ree-range, **L**ocal, **O**rganic, and **W**hole foods. Regarding relative proportions of food items, a variety of colorful vegetables and fruits should be the stars of the show.

Many experts suggest limiting our eating window to ten hours per day or less, and to stop eating at least four hours before bedtime. To improve digestion, it is also best to chew food slowly and thoroughly.

This meal plan should serve only as a general outline, designed for individuals who have no significant medical problems. Best practices often change over time, so it is important that all individuals stay up-to-date on current recommendations.

People with conditions such as diabetes or autoimmune disease may need to make adjustments to the above plan. Those with digestion issues may also need to make modifications; as may those who have food allergies or intolerances. Individuals with these conditions, or any other significant medical problem, should consult a Registered Dietician for individually-tailored dietary advice.

Enjoy Blissful Slumber

It is important that we recharge our bodies with plenty of sleep each night. Sleeping well is absolutely one of the best ways to optimize health, longevity, and happiness. It's free, it feels good, and it requires no effort. A good night of sleep improves cognition, memory, mood, heart health, athletic performance, and immune response.

The amount of sleep a person requires is highly individualized, but most individuals perform best if they get somewhere between seven and eight hours of sleep each night. Routinely averaging less than six hours of sleep (or more than nine hours) has been correlated with poorer health. If we don't feel energetic, or if we always seem to need caffeine to get us going, it is often because we need more sleep.

Tips for Restful Sleep to Consider:

-Follow a consistent sleep schedule (many experts consider this to be the most important of all sleep tips). Go to bed at roughly the same time every evening, and get up at about the same time every morning.

-Keep bedrooms cool and dark, but be sure to allow natural light to come through the windows every morning. Spend at least half an hour outside in sunlight every day, which helps trigger our bodies to sleep better at night.

-Avoid caffeinated products after the lunch-time meal – this includes coffee, many types of sodas and teas, and chocolate. A short early afternoon nap can be reinvigorating for many people, but try to avoid napping anytime beyond mid-afternoon.

-Daily exercise improves sleep, but it is best for most people to avoid strenuous exercise within a couple hours of bedtime.

-Avoid falling asleep on a couch or chair in the evening before getting up to go to bed, as this lowers the level of a chemical substance (adenosine) in our bloodstream that builds up each day and helps induce sleep. Keep the lights low in the evening. Turn off all screens at least one hour before bedtime.

-If you have concerns that weigh heavily on your mind, consider writing them down, and then leaving the piece of paper in the kitchen. The challenges will still be there tomorrow – no need to worry about them tonight.

-In the last hour before bedtime, consider doing something relaxing and uplifting; perhaps reading about your hobbies, or listening to some soothing music. You may wish to conclude the evening with a short meditation or prayer of gratitude, and a conscious smile. It is then time to close your eyes…and drift off into blissful slumber.

Use It or Lose It

As with many things in life, it is useful to consider exercise from an evolutionary perspective. Most things make more sense when viewed through the lens of evolution. Of note, belief in evolution certainly does not invalidate belief in a Creator – one who may have designed our universe and all its wondrous creatures to naturally evolve.

Millions of years in the making, human bodies are still most suited for a life of hunting and gathering. Therefore, if we wish to achieve optimal health and happiness, it is imperative that we imitate the physicality of the lives of our hunter-gatherer ancestors – working our bodies like the athletes they are designed to be.

When gathering food and water, our ancient predecessors frequently ambled many miles at a leisurely pace. When tracking game, they walked more quickly, and would also run when necessary. Oftentimes the chase necessitated putting forth extreme and maximal effort, sometimes even culminating in a life-or-death brawl with their quarry. And, if they were successful in their endeavor, they used physical strength to carry their bounty back to camp.

Today we can roughly approximate our ancestors' physical activities in a more modern fashion. We can take a daily walk to imitate food gathering ventures. We can augment this routine a few times per week with a brisker walking pace, sometimes adding in a run or bicycle ride in place of tracking and following game. Our routine can also occasionally include short bursts of high-level exertion, such as running fast or riding our bicycle up a hill once or twice per week – in place of bringing down a large animal. Add in some moderate weight training a few times per week, and we are now ready to hunt and gather with the best of them.

Exercise improves not only our physical health, but our mental health as well. People who regularly exercise demonstrate improved confidence, better sleep patterns, lower levels of anxiety and depression, slower rates of cognitive decline, and – as you may have guessed – greater levels of happiness. Major health advisories recommend at least 30 minutes of aerobic exercise 5 days per week, and at least 2 days of muscle resistance training per week.

A human body is like a lot of things in life; we *use* it or we *lose* it. If we do not remain physically active, it is as if the universe thinks it no longer needs us. Our physical body may then begin to prematurely self-destruct and decay back into the Earth – dust to dust.

Note: It is important to check with a medical care provider before beginning any new exercise routine. Always start slowly with gentle exercise before working up to more strenuous sessions.

Stretch Daily

For optimal health and well-being, it is helpful to include stretching in our daily routines. Stretching lowers the risk of musculoskeletal injury, decreases blood pressure, improves posture, and even helps alleviate stress and chronic pain.

Gentle dynamic stretching is helpful before a workout; however, most stretching should be done after a warmup, as cold muscles can be injured by excessive stretching. After a workout or short warm-up, *all* muscle groups should be stretched; holding each stretching position for roughly thirty seconds.

Stretching should be performed gently and slowly, and never to the point of pain – it should always feel good. Even warmed-up muscles can be damaged by over-stretching.

If desired, quiet meditation can be easily incorporated into a stretching program. This can start by focusing on breathing patterns; paying close attention to the sensation of air moving through our nostrils with each breath.

Slow and gentle movement, such as with dance, yoga, or Tai Chi, can also be intermixed into a routine. Softly-played background music may help provide additional relaxation.

A reasonable goal to consider is a dedicated 10-20-minute session of meditative stretching and slow movement each day. If at times this is not possible, it is advisable to at least take a minute or two, every few hours or so, to walk about and perform some gentle stretches.

The ideas offered above can help build a strong body – a ship sturdy enough to last a lifetime.

Next to be explored are strategies that can help create a strong mind – opening our sails to the powerful winds of knowledge, imagination, and character.

FIVE
Unfurling the Sails

ONE OF HUMANKIND'S most noteworthy figures is the late great physicist, Albert Einstein. Although most of us are familiar with his scientific endeavors and famous equations (like $e=mc^2$), many people may not be aware that he was a gifted philosopher as well.

Einstein once said:

"You can never solve a problem on the level it was created."

When considering how this applies to humanity's many challenges, Einstein's words can mean that *solutions* to problems born of self-interest or unawareness must arise from higher levels of selfless transcendent thought – i.e., when others go low, we must go high.

A transcendent person knows that optimal *individual* happiness is imbedded within the greater fabric of collective *global* happiness. They know that local personal actions often create ripple effects that may impact citizens on the other side of our planet – even a thousand years from now. And they know that the actions of distant global inhabitants may affect us as well; today and in the future.

Again, the individual, the collective, and the Earth itself – *Person, People, and Planet* – are equal and inseparable, in time and in space. Embracing this overarching ideal helps potentiate the elements of a strong and resilient mind. With this general precept as a background, three important foundations of a robust mind will be examined: *Knowledge, Imagination, and Character.*

Knowledge and Imagination

"Imagination is more important than knowledge."

The above famous quote by Albert Einstein (there are many) was not likely meant to diminish the importance of knowledge. No, far from it. Imagination may sometimes be thought of as flashes of inspiration and brilliance – often seemingly arising out of nothingness – but it is much more than that.

Einstein could not have dreamed up his ground-breaking theories without an extensive background in mathematics and physics. Knowledge is a crucial part of the creative process. Indeed, imagination springs forth from rich repositories of knowledge – and releases the power of it.

It is important that each of us gain as much knowledge as our neural connections can possibly accept. Knowledge is power. It is the creative synthesis of the efforts and achievements of our ancestors; the sum of their successes and failures. Integrated and applied knowledge creates a foundation for *imagination*; which, as Einstein noted, is perhaps even more powerful than knowledge itself.

Imagination arises from a fount of integrated knowledge accrued over a lifetime. And it does this best when emanating from the mind of a transcendent individual – one who wishes to become a meaningful part of something greater than themself, choosing to use their knowledge to help achieve the global greater good.

It is imperative that each of us gather up as much knowledge as we possibly can – and then make full use of our imagination. *Imagination and knowledge potentiate the effects of each other.*

We must imagine ways to create a sustainable planet; with bountiful oceans, wild forests, clean air, and rich soils. We must imagine a world of peaceful, happy, and healthy citizens; with liberty and justice for all.

We must dream often, and we must dream big…and then we must take action.

Character

Making noble dreams come true requires both knowledge and imagination – and usually strength of character as well. Some character qualities to consider are these: *positivity, loyalty, hope,* and *forgiveness.*

Positivity

> "The mind is its own place, and in itself can make a heaven of hell, a hell of heaven."
> -John Milton, Paradise Lost

An event typically has no meaning other than the meaning we choose to assign it. In many circumstances, we humans have the ability to think of an experience or challenge in any way we wish; and it is within our power to generally hold a positive outlook.

That said, there are rare tragic life events that hold no apparent positive aspects, no matter how we do the math. Sometimes truly terrible things do happen, and there is often no making sense of them – nor are there any discernible silver linings.

If you are a person upon whom a great tragedy has befallen, it is my deep regret that humankind cannot together carry your pain; if only for a moment, to give you rest.

We may truly lack the words to diminish your anguish and grief. We can only attempt to accept a measure of your great sorrow; sharing your tears with you, so you are not alone. We can admire your courage and strength, as you resolutely move forward, carrying with you the great weight of emptiness. And we can pray that your burden will soon be lightened, and that you will once again find peace and happiness.

It is essential to differentiate between truly catastrophic events over which we have no control, and the much more frequent daily life events of lesser magnitude; challenges that are more easily addressed by utilizing positive thought processes of grit and determination.

It is perhaps part of human nature to sometimes excessively focus on the negative, and downplay the positive, even in regards to relatively commonplace events. After all, humankind seems to be evolutionarily predisposed to think this way – probably because negative outcomes could easily hurt or kill our early hunter-gatherer ancestors, while positive outcomes often only made their lives modestly better. It is important to be aware of our subconscious human predispositions, as they are not always well-suited for a modern world.

We humans have the capacity to influence our own thoughts, and to create our own reality; even at a cellular, chemically-mediated level. And we can do this by choosing to shape our perceptions of the stimuli that enter our consciousness. Purposeful, focused, positive thinking can truly modify the neural connections and chemical milieu of the brain – which is really quite astonishing.

Positive thinking can help our mind to strengthen itself – by naturally altering the levels of our neurotransmitters, and also by creating (or selectively pruning) neural pathways to increase our level of happiness.

It is generally within our capabilities to think positively; *choosing* to build better neural connections, strengthening our minds to the highest possible level. The intent here is not to whitewash reality, rather to consider it in a different light. We can choose to favor a narrative composed of *optimistic* thoughts and words; cognitively reframing problems into challenges, and challenges into opportunities.

…And, we can also choose to *accept* that which is unchangeable.

Acceptance

To achieve optimal individual well-being, many thought leaders note that it is imperative to accept the things we cannot change – and to find the courage to change the things we can and should.

We cannot change events that happened in the past, some for which we may bear personal responsibility, and others that are outside our control. Although we may be unable to change certain life events or personal circumstances, we can always change our responses to them – and sometimes *acceptance* is the most positive response.

Acceptance can certainly be difficult to attain. In some terrible circumstances, acceptance may be nearly impossible to completely embrace, and it may always be accompanied by an element of pain.

In less tragic instances, acceptance may come more easily if we consider that our struggles often provide us the opportunity to create our better selves. Our responses to both triumph and tragedy help make us who we are.

I once listened to a courageous young teenager with severe sickle cell disease say he never spent time wishing he had been born differently – because his medical condition helped make him into the person he is today.

Human rights activist Desmond Tutu said we can choose to be either ennobled or embittered by our struggles. We must choose to be *ennobled* – and perhaps consider using our painful experiences to help others who face struggles similar to our own.

If we are angry/anxious/depressed about the state of the world, we must rise above that, acknowledging the extraordinary potential of humankind to overcome challenges. Our collective problems are all solvable, and positive *thoughts* beget positive *outcomes*.

In the pages to follow, many daunting challenges will be discussed. The viability of our planet and the lives of its inhabitants are truly at risk. This is not hyperbole. If we are to avoid tremendous suffering, changes must be made swiftly.

It is imperative that we not lose heart, or acquiesce to ruminations of poor outcomes. *We must stay positive.* And we can know that humankind is making great progress in several areas.

In the last few decades, we have had tremendous success in decreasing early childhood mortality, and also in lifting many disadvantaged populations out of poverty. We have created miraculous new vaccines to prevent disease, and novel tools and medications to diagnose and treat many illnesses. We have also rehabilitated vast areas of environmentally ravaged landscapes – such as the Loess plateau in China, the Panamanian rain forest, and the massive Gorongosa National Park in Africa.

Worldwide, there are innumerable individuals and coalitions working to create a better world – by providing education, sustainable agriculture and energy, equitable distribution of food/water/health care, and financial assistance to those who need it. The challenges are immense, but our efforts are paying off.

A peaceful, just, and sustainable planet is an absolutely attainable dream. Sustainable Global Happiness is well within our reach – it just takes great willpower and work to achieve, individually and collectively.

Today, it is as if we have each been given the opportunity to become a superhero. We can literally help save the world. It is not too late. We must not wring our hands and imagine poor outcomes; rather we must roll up our sleeves and get to work – and do so cheerfully and with great confidence.

We can *choose* to be a positive person. Like author Stephen Covey said, we can bring our own sunny weather. Positivity is contagious.

We can try to find something uplifting to smile and laugh about every day, even in times of challenge. We can decide to look for the good – knowing that we see what we look for.

We can choose to live a life of great Happiness; deciding to be optimistic about our personal future, and the future of our planet and all its inhabitants. We can write our positive expectations down on paper, and also say them aloud. Many prophecies are self-fulfilling – we start to believe our own stories, you know.

We can create a vision of ourselves in the future, surrounded by family and friends on a lush and beautiful planet; where all people are treated equally, every person has enough to eat, and all citizens live together as one – as brothers and sisters in peace.

Loyalty

> "We men and women are all in the same boat upon a stormy sea. We owe to each other a terrible and tragic loyalty."
> -G.K. Chesterton

We owe our loyalty to all of humanity; the mass aggregate of all past, present, and future inhabitants of our planet. And it is to noble principles that guide and protect humankind, that we also owe our allegiance.

It is essential to favor loyalty to honorable values and the greater good over blind loyalty to individuals or organizations. Pledging lifelong allegiance to an individual person or political party can be fraught with danger, because loyalty to and from others must be earned anew each day.

It is important to embrace and regard the message far more than the messenger. People and parties change, culture and circumstances shift, and even the best of men and women may stumble and fall when the storm is upon them – whereas, noble principles stand forever firm against the elements.

Hope

> "Hope springs eternal."
> -Alexander Pope

It is important to never give up hope. Hope that there is some grand reason for our magnificent universe – and each of our personal existences within it. Hope that humankind will continue to make the effort to realize the fullness of our extraordinary potential. Hope that the great powers of love and forgiveness will triumph over resentment, aggression, and tyranny.

We can have hope in a greater Presence or purpose. Hope in something that is far greater than ourselves.

Forgiveness

> "If you want to see the brave, look to those who can return love for hatred. If you want to see the heroic, look to those who can forgive." -The Bhagavad Gita

If humankind is to fully thrive, we must all forgive and be forgiven. No individual (or nation) is perfect. We are all in need of forgiveness – and forgiveness is perhaps the greatest manifestation of love.

Forgiveness requires great strength. It takes tremendous power to release the bonds of bitterness, resentment, and revenge that anchor us to unhappiness. We must summon our strength to sever such cords of discontent – and then sail away with a new lightness of spirit.

Forgiveness brings peace. Forgiveness sets us free.

PART III

The Challenges Ahead

SIX

First Things First

EARTH IS AN exquisite paradise, where beauty and abundance can be found at nearly every turn. Our planet's ecosystems presently offer most of humanity enough food to eat, clean water to drink, and materials to build warm and safe homes. But, of course, the world is not all rainbows and butterflies…

Today, hundreds of millions of global citizens are hungry, cold, or sick; in large part because our planet's treasures are not equitably distributed, but also because there are simply becoming too many of us living here. Adding to this problem, the ecosystems that yield healthy food and clean water are not being sustainably maintained. This could portend even more suffering in the future, if changes are not quickly made.

There are also many global citizens ruled by brutally oppressive leaders; thuggish types who shamelessly violate human rights, using intimidation and violence to maintain domination. Even in democratic countries like the US, principles of social and environmental justice are sometimes trampled over by powerful people in a mad rush for even more money and power.

The goal of Sustainable Global Happiness does not imply an existence without struggles, rather one of overcoming challenges to reach this ideal.

Every challenge that humankind faces must be considered with our ultimate destination clearly in mind. When considering any new path that humanity may embark upon – be it that of a new technology, cultural transformation, or government decree – we must always ask this question: "Will this path lead to lasting global happiness on a sustainable Earth?"

If the answer is no, then we must find ourselves a better way.

Humanity's Challenges: Daunting, but Solvable

We live in extraordinary times. Humankind is presently faced with several simultaneous challenges: A recent devastating global pandemic; economic uncertainties; cultural and political tensions at a boiling point; massive wealth discrepancies; widespread geopolitical skirmishes; a renewed nuclear-arms race; and many more – all under the specter of climate change and severe environmental degradation.

Separately, these challenges each have the power to be generation-defining events. Together, they potentiate each other, coalescing into a superstorm that darkens the skies over a global populace often at war with itself.

Humankind is not presently addressing its challenges from a point of action and unity. Instead, posturing nations stare each other down, beating their chests while displaying mighty military arsenals in grand parades and naval brigades. Meanwhile, their own citizens often fight bitterly amongst themselves. Even in the US, a country rich with incredible bounty, we act as onlookers or participants in a vicious fight between the political left and right – with the fate of democracy and the lives of future global citizens possibly hanging in the balance.

Some people speak about our current situation in apocalyptic terms, even suggesting that human beings are characters of a story in its final chapters. We must never succumb to this pessimistic way of thinking – because, as noted, prophecies can sometimes be self-fulfilling.

The complex organism that is humanity is indeed suffering, but it suffers from an autoimmune disease; attacking itself from within, rather than fighting the true ills that it faces. Individually, we remain self-focused; collectively, we are thus often torn asunder.

Still, the imminent demise of humankind is quite unlikely – we are the captains of our own destiny, and we have weathered many rough storms before. Our challenges are daunting, to be sure, but each one is quite solvable. We just need to get out of our own way.

Prioritizing Present Challenges

If humankind wishes to realize its full potential of Sustainable Global Happiness, it is vitally important that we prioritize present challenges in terms of their impact on the survival of our species. We must put first things first.

To that end, it is critical to understand that *without a peaceful and sustainable planet, nothing else is possible.* We must choose leaders who consistently acknowledge and interweave this principle into every policy decision – and we must individually embrace this ideal ourselves.

The fate of humanity is wholly dependent on a safe, sustainable, and regenerative planet. Existential threats to our species, such as global nuclear war, or widespread disease and crop failures from climate change and environmental degradation, must not be relegated to the back-burner. World peace and a healthy planet are bedrock elements of humanity's continued existence.

The Bulletin of the Atomic Scientists notes that the Doomsday Clock is at its historic most extreme, including during the time of the Cold War. Our land-based nuclear missile launching systems are on hair-trigger alert, creating an immediate existential risk to humanity.

Computer or human error could falsely indicate an incoming missile attack, and a massive nuclear response could be initiated – with a real counter-attack retaliation after that. In an instant, nearly all major cities of the adversary nations would be obliterated into radioactive ash. Millions of people living near blast epicenters would be killed immediately, while millions more living at the margins would perish over the ensuing weeks, succumbing to slow and painful deaths from massive burns and radiation poisoning.

The rest of the world would suffer greatly as well, as the ensuing widespread fires and smoke could shield the Sun, resulting in a "nuclear winter" – causing massive global crop failures and famine.

Some world leaders have the sole authority to launch nuclear weapons at a moment's notice – this at a time when international diplomacy is in great need of repair. In 2019, the US pulled out of the Cold War-era Intermediate-Range Nuclear Forces Treaty (INF) with Russia, accusing them of violating the pact by deploying a nuclear-capable cruise missile that could reach European cities in minutes.

At the time of this writing, Russia has invaded Ukraine – and has threatened the possible use of nuclear weapons, even against any country that intervenes. Both East and West have been resuming a massive nuclear-weapons buildup; reversing the policies of many administrations since the Cold War.

And then there is the slow burn, the more insidious existential risk of planetary environmental collapse. Over the last few years, the world has literally been on fire. The effects of climate change and poor environmental practices have caused vast swaths of land to burn; ranging from the enormous coniferous forests of Siberia to the tropical jungles of the Amazon basin. Millions of acres were also scorched in Australia, where a billion animals have perished. We are currently witnessing widespread devastation of life and property from wildfires in Canada and the western United States as well.

Globally, several Earth species are becoming extinct each day. Coral reefs are dying from heat stress and seawater acidification from carbon dioxide emissions. Millions of years in the making, business as usual will result in the demise of these ancient creatures.

Coral reefs provide habitat to over twenty-five percent of marine species, and all global citizens have some level of dependence upon them. Astonishingly, the coral will be all but gone by the end of this century, if drastic changes are not made.

We must get this right. Future generations may swim blissfully alongside diverse schools of fish, meandering through pristine colonies of colorful coral – and be grateful for our foresight. Or, they may curse us for our apathy; as they look upon masses of jellyfish, one of the few species left to float above the bleached white skeletons of coral creatures forever gone.

Land masses are not faring any better than the seas. Glyphosate herbicide and other pesticides are present in much of the food we eat and drink. The numbers of pollinators and other beneficial insects are plummeting; imperiling our future food supply even more. Our air, water, and soil continue to be poisoned by pollution and pesticides.

Bruised and bloodied by relentless assaults upon imperiled ecosystems, a falling Earth cannot forever sustain a rising populace. Tethered firmly together, *Person, People and Planet* ultimately trace the same curve, destined to experience a similar fate.

It takes a safe and healthy planet to create a healthy human. This is not a red-state fact, or a blue-state fact; it is simply a fact. It is important to remember this when choosing our leaders and casting our ballots.

Whether an individual's major issue of concern is personal liberty or collective justice; open borders or closed borders; more or fewer gun laws; more or fewer abortion restrictions; more socialism or more capitalism – or just about anything else – none of these issues would likely matter as much to inhabitants of a dying planet completely engulfed in a war with itself. Peace and environmental sustainability are *primary* issues.

Presently, it is as if we are all travelers on the Titanic, arguing over the dinner menu instead of watching out for icebergs. We must prioritize our challenges. *Without a safe and healthy planet, nothing else is possible.*

This is not to say that issues other than peace and environmental sustainability are irrelevant today. Citizens care very much about humankind's other problems, too – and rightly so. In the following chapter we will examine some of the core values that influence our thinking and behavior regarding our many present global challenges.

SEVEN

Core Values

MANY OF HUMANKIND'S domestic and international disagreements are related to our personal values regarding **tribalism**, **spirituality/religion**, **liberty**, and **justice**. Human beings don't need to always agree with one other, but we do need to understand the paths each other have taken to get to where we are today – acknowledging the triumphs and tragedies of each other's experiential lives.

With this understanding, we can more easily come together to collaborate and compromise, seeking joint solutions to some of the more vexing issues that humankind faces today. Let's now examine a few elements of human value systems that sometimes drive us apart.

Tribe Loyalty

When we think about our love of country, we should ask ourselves "Am I a patriot, or am I a nationalist?" There is a difference.

A patriot loves the citizens, culture, and noble ideals of their country. A nationalist loves their country – no matter what. There is great danger in this latter way of thinking. A nation must *earn* the allegiance of its citizens anew each day, continually engaging in actions that are kind, just, and noble.

Patriots apologize for their mistakes – and then they make things right. They wish to maintain their country's position of global leadership through hard work, collaboration, and innovation; offering a hand up to their competitors, not a boot on the throat.

Patriots demonstrate the courage to break rank if necessary, demanding good character of their fellow citizens and leaders – whereas, nationalists unfailingly march in rank and file, often to an unmeritorious life, or sometimes death.

There is certainly nothing wrong with winning – as long as the game is played on a level playing field. A true patriot is willing to expand their notion of tribe, striving to help their country become *the first among equals.*

In the US, there are currently warring factions even within our own tribe. We often see this in our government institutions, where some leaders, on both sides of the aisle, seemingly retreat behind party lines as a matter of course. Often choosing to vote as a united group, some of our politicians appear to value loyalty to party and self over loyalty to principle and the greater good.

Perhaps at a subconscious level, many of us, their constituents, have learned to do the same thing.

Spirituality

Some of us gain inspiration and ideals from an abiding religious faith – which may indeed be a wonderful guiding light. And noble principles, espoused beneath the glow of stained-glass windows, often carry far beyond cathedral walls.

If we were to ask citizens around the world to choose the religion that follows the truest spiritual path, we would likely receive many different answers. Yet there is a key commonality between various faith groups. Indeed, a central tenet of nearly every major religion is this:

"Do unto others, as you would have them do unto you."

Some form of this Golden Rule exists in every major faith. And this precept does not specify that "others" includes only individuals from one's own church, community, or nation.

"Others" includes *all* people – at home *and* abroad, today *and* tomorrow. A truly spiritual person strives to create social justice for all present generations, and to help preserve our planet for the benefit of all future global inhabitants as well.

Liberty

Most of us say that we cherish the ideals of "liberty" and "justice." We may sometimes even recite these words at the end of the US Pledge of Allegiance saying, "…with liberty and justice for all." However, even though liberty and justice (freedom and fairness) are each noble ideals, they sometimes work at cross purposes. We must often give up a measure of liberty if we want more justice, and we may have to sacrifice a bit of justice if we want more liberty.

Nobody likes their government to tell them what to do. We all want the freedom to do as we please. However, exercising this liberty may not always be fair to others. For example, if we choose to forgo hand-washing, sanitation, masking, or social distancing during a deadly disease outbreak, we may be putting other people's lives at risk. The small increase in our personal liberty is thus offset by a large decrease in justice to our fellow citizens.

Still, we want our government to mostly leave us alone to do as we please…or do we?

Come to think of it, most of us don't want the police and fire departments to leave us alone if our house is burglarized or is on fire. We don't want our military personnel to leave us alone if our nation is attacked. We don't want government planners, engineers, and builders to leave us alone to construct our own bridges, roads, airports, libraries, and schools. And we don't want government social workers and advocates to leave us alone if we are an individual who happens to be born on the left side of the Bell curve of fairness.

Nobody likes government overreach. But if we wish to live in an amazing nation, such as the US or other great democracy, we cannot always have our way – we must often surrender a small portion of our personal liberty for the good of the collective.

If we want to get something, we have to give something. There is no free lunch.

Justice

Most people would say they believe in the idea of fairness or "social justice." However, each of us has a different definition of fairness – and we are usually most aware of how fairness impacts us personally, and less concerned about fairness as it relates to other people.

Present generations must often take responsibility for the actions of our predecessors. "That's not fair," you say? Well, it is also not fair that our children and grandchildren will have to pay back a national debt that we in present generations have been a part of creating.

It may not be fair that some people receive more social benefits than others; especially if they might not work as hard, do not have a similar level of education, or have not taken as many financial risks in their lives.

But it also may not be fair if a person or their ancestors were perhaps born citizens inside the borders of the US or other rich democracy; bequeathed a birthright they did not earn, allowing them to live a life more luxurious than the vast majority of global inhabitants born outside such borders, no matter how hard they work.

Consider a refugee-parent today, fleeing a deadly regime with malnourished children in tow, and no money for food to feed them. Or a young Black woman or man suddenly freed from an American plantation in 1865, possessing only the clothes on their back and perhaps no highly profitable skills. Now imagine these people attempting to create a financial legacy for their children or future descendants, often in the face of persistent discrimination. Not an impossible task; but extremely difficult, nonetheless.

It is a complex balancing act; determining how far societies must go to correct present and prior injustices, attempting to address the needs of every global citizen. Presently, we may have to extend our timescale a bit; perhaps bending the reed of fairness for another decade or two, hoping to create a just tomorrow for all – even if that sometimes possibly entails sacrificing a small amount of individual fairness today.

We live in a world where fairness was never promised. Collectively, we just do our best to come as close to fair as possible, knowing that we can perhaps never quite reach this ideal. A worthy aim for humanity would be to ensure equality of *opportunity* for every global citizen – but not necessarily equality of *outcome* for all.

We will come back again to liberty and justice in the pages to follow, as these two notions are at the heart of many societal challenges.

Comprehensive solutions to humanity's challenges can certainly not be provided in these relatively few pages. But it is possible to perform a reconnaissance flyover mission, obtaining a general lay-of-the-land; knowing that each issue will require a follow-up deep dive, at which point further discussion can lead to equitable solutions via collaboration and compromise.

Knowing where we came from as a species, recognizing the potential biases in our individual value systems, and developing a clear vision of our collective destination are all essential elements for creating Sustainable Global Happiness.

With this understanding as a background, the next few chapters will examine a selection of humankind's present challenges – and attempt to do so from an unbiased central vantage point.

EIGHT
Meet Me in the Middle

IT IS IMPERATIVE that global citizens thoughtfully consider all sides of vexing challenges, and to do so from a position of apolitical and passionate centrism – even if we happen to be registered with a specific political party.

For a person to be centrist does not mean to be lukewarm or wishy-washy about important issues. No, not at all. Rather, it means to realize that most problems are multifaceted and complex, and that opposing factions each usually have valid points to consider.

Although it has proven durable, one problem with the essentially two-party US political system is that each faction takes stances on disparate issues that sometimes seem to be based more on cultural precedent and party loyalty than on logic and consistency.

In addition, solutions to a wide array of complex issues are often reduced to a simple binary choice; one where loyal party members must accept views that are often diametrically opposed to those of the competing party. To toe the party line, one must often be fully *for* or *against* an issue – even if the best answer starts with "it depends…"

Some citizens wish to resolutely choose sides, sometimes becoming deeply entrenched in party identity, perhaps because there is perceived safety in being a member of a group. It may also be in our genetic makeup to grow closer together by seeking a common enemy, perhaps satisfying a subconscious desire for competition and victory.

Two-party systems can thus engender fierce partisanship; inclining members to retaliate tit-for-tat to real or perceived attacks from those on the other side – at times escalating into battles of distrust and revenge where there are no real winners. Recall Mahatma Gandhi's admonition: "An eye for an eye leaves the whole world blind."

The term "centrism" can be confusing, because some people may consider it to be an automatic default to a non-thinking and dispirited middle ground compromise – which it is not. Centrism means to demonstrate the courage to do the right thing, even if fellow citizens and party members don't agree with you.

Although a centrist seeks reconciliation, compromise, and peace, a philosophy of centrism does not mean to take a precise center position on every issue. It means that, *on average*, a centrist's views are positioned somewhere in a broad middle ground; because some of their ideals may be endorsed by the political left, and some by the right. It means they attempt to use independent thinking, logic, and principle when deciding where they stand on an issue – irrespective of which party endorses their view.

A centrist person believes both sides often make valid points. However, importantly, they do not necessarily assign moral or logical *equivalence* to each opposing view. The optimal solution is usually located somewhere between the two factions – but often not precisely on the fifty-yard line.

A more exact term for "centrist" might be "independent," although this can be confused with the Independent Party, which has its own platform. Another option is the term "apolitical," but that may imply apathy to some people. Identifying oneself as a "non-affiliated voter" can also be a good description.

Perhaps the best description of all is "Passionate Centrism," meaning the ideal of enthusiastically seeking logic-based and politically-unbiased solutions to achieve the greater good.

Finding common ground can take time and patience, especially in present times. A moving pendulum does not suddenly stop in the middle. The further it swings to one side, the more it will swing to the opposite extreme – and the longer it will take to reach a state of equilibrium.

Finding common ground also often necessitates marching into dangerous territory. Tempers sometimes run hot, and belligerents on each side can seem to be looking for a fight with anyone who will not unfailingly wave their flag. Many believe that if you are not always with them, you are against them. Centrists can therefore potentially face the wrath of two parties rather than just one.

Nevertheless, it is imperative that every citizen demonstrates the courage and fortitude to venture into the messy and uncomfortable middle. It is also important to enter the fray as agents of peace; fighting only against humankind's present challenges – and not against each other. The opponent is simply the challenge itself.

Presently, with many nations so divided, compromise is absolutely essential. Each side must be willing to make concessions they may find personally or politically unsavory. Today, there are some individuals, many of whom are political leaders, who are often unwilling to compromise. They believe the other side to be too irrational – perhaps not realizing their foes think the exact same of them. They thus refuse to negotiate; and it is here they make a grievous error.

Failure to engage in respectful dialogue and compromise can be a precursor to aggression, even armed aggression. And it can sometimes lead to civil war. There is always a chance of that in any country of course – even in the US. It has happened before. If that possibility does not alarm us, it should. Democracy is a fragile experiment, and it could all go sideways in an instant.

No person or party should expect everything to go their way. Some people think if they give up a little, they are at a greater risk of giving up a lot. They are mistaken. A person is more likely to lose *everything*, if they are unwilling to compromise on *anything* – whether it is their views on guns, immigration, socialism, or anything else.

If we refuse to compromise, and we push our adversaries hard enough, they may indeed go away. But probably only for a while. We will likely see them again – and the next time they may be brandishing torches and pitchforks.

We must find common ground before it is too late to avert greater conflict. It is essential that we confront our vexing problems head on, before they get worse. It is much easier to put out a match than a wildfire.

Warning bells are ringing. Presently, some political leaders openly speak crassly of others, failing to respect the sanctity of their elected office, and setting a very poor example for their constituents. Some have even encouraged violence toward their political opponents.

Today, there are millions of global citizens forced to exist in hovels or refugee camps lacking adequate food, water, and medical care. Many of these people also face recurrent danger of bodily harm from fellow citizens or their own government, particularly if they voice an unsanctioned opinion.

Meanwhile, by way of comparison, many of the rest of us eat three fine meals of delicious and abundant food each day – and often dessert, too. We enjoy the freedom to do or say nearly whatever we please, without fear of violent retribution by our governments. We drive nice automobiles, wear beautiful clothes, and frequently attend sporting events or other entertainment venues. Each night, we drift off to sleep in a comfortable bed, tucked away in the safety of our own homes.

Yet some of us, across the political spectrum, at home and abroad, still act greatly aggrieved. A few even glorify the idea of violence, somehow deeming differing views on issues such as immigration, pandemic responses, environmentalism – or even religion – as worthy of eliciting physical aggression, or even armed insurrection.

Some of our citizens and leaders, again on both sides of the political divide, spread false narratives that demonize their political opponents – inflammatory words that can turn disagreements into arguments, and arguments into insurrections. Insurrections can soon evolve into outright war. And, of course, war quickly descends into hell.

Sometimes it only takes one spark, one irrational person, to ignite a tremendous explosion. World War I was triggered by a single event (the assassination of Archduke Franz Ferdinand and his wife Sophie) that quickly blew up into a war that engulfed the planet.

Victors of war do not emerge unscathed. No one truly ever wins a war; they merely survive it. War is sheer terror and dread. War is the arms and legs of young men and women soldiers blown off their bodies. War is seared flesh laid bare, and the acrid smell of decay. War is the final frightened cry of a bullet-torn son or daughter, dying alone; far away from home. War is an innocent infant child caught in mortar crossfire; whose tiny, fragile body is burned beyond recognition.

War is the tortured, heaving, hollowed sobs of grief-stricken parents with no tears left to cry – forced to forever endure the unimaginable.

"It is only those who have neither fired a shot or heard the shrieks and groans of the wounded who cry aloud for blood, for vengeance, for desolation. War is hell."
–Union General William Tecumseh Sherman

Throughout history, many malevolent actors have attempted to tear away humankind's thin cloak of civility, a mantle hard-won over millennia. About eighty years ago, Adolph Hitler once again exposed humanity's red teeth and claws, convincing many of his nation's citizens to condone the unspeakable.

Today, the world still witnesses horrible brutality in several regions – as with Russia's invasion of Ukraine, the wars in Yemen and Sudan, and the Israel-Palestine conflict. Much of humankind still possesses a wild inner core, where self-serving instincts run strong.

Presently, in the US and worldwide, there are politicians, pundits and citizens, on each end of the political spectrum, who wish to again summon forth dark demons; sowing seeds of fear, mistrust, confusion, and doubt. They are playing with fire; risking war and terrible sorrow.

And for what? Because they are not rich enough? Because they think that life is not fair? Our differences are not worth screaming and lying for. And they are certainly not worth killing or dying for.

We must not be swayed by angry outlier leaders and commentators, or their fawning constituents and listeners, who often search for selfish gains.

Equally disconcerting as the heated words of the provocateurs, is the chilling silence of multitudes of their fellow party members; those who refuse to condemn the inflammatory words and actions of radicalized political colleagues and leaders.

By remaining mute, many citizens and leaders of otherwise good character may truly believe they are exhibiting an admirable quality of party unity. However, what they are often instead demonstrating is complicity with ignoble principles and incivility. They are also displaying a momentary lapse of the honor, courage, and selflessness that perhaps once propelled them into a life of service to the greater good. By so doing, they are putting the tenuous experiment of democracy at great risk.

It is essential that all of us, leaders and constituents of every stripe, work together for the greater global good. When necessary, we must be strong enough to stand up and challenge even those who are members of our own ranks. And we must be intelligent and tough enough to seek collaboration and compromise with fellow citizens who may think differently than us.

We can demonstrate calmness and warmth when discussing our differences. We can listen intently with an open mind and heart, and soften our edges a bit. We can meet somewhere in the middle.

The middle road is a wide road, with plenty of room for all.

NINE

Bridging Our Great Divides

MANY OF THE challenges we face today are concerns we would rather not think about; or at least not frequently discuss with others. The topics are often inherently uncomfortable, and disagreements can lead to disharmony at both personal and collective levels. It is far less socially dangerous to talk about football and the weather.

Nevertheless, it is essential that we jump into the fray – because a future of Sustainable Global Happiness depends on it.

Cognitive dissonance theory posits that a person is not completely at ease if they simultaneously hold two or more conflicting beliefs. If one wishes to attain psychological equilibrium, it is often necessary to either *ignore*, *refute*, or *alter* one of the competing beliefs.

As discussed in chapter seven, most people strongly value both liberty (freedom) and justice (fairness). However, as noted, these two ideals are often at odds with each other. Having the freedom to do whatever one wishes is not always entirely just (fair) to others. As is said, a person may indeed have the liberty to swing their fist – but that freedom ends just before reaching another person's nose.

Which ideal shall we favor – liberty, or justice? How do we reconcile these opposing (yet worthy) factors that have the potential to create such cognitive dissonance and discomfort? Which ideal shall we ignore or refute…or perhaps alter?

Choosing one meritorious entity or ideal entirely over the other can sometimes be a betrayal of one of our individual core values – either that of liberty or justice – which can cause us to experience internal conflict. So, which shall we choose?

It appears that it is part of human nature to often take the easiest way; perhaps because it is part of our genetic makeup to conserve energy when possible. Regarding liberty and justice, a person can choose the path of least resistance, deciding to either refute or ignore one of the dissonant factors, defaulting completely to the stronger of their personal core values – which may be liberty, or may be justice.

They convince themself that this is not really a betrayal, as they are sacrificing something that they perhaps consciously or subconsciously choose to not recognize as being important. They therefore attempt to settle into a quiet state; one that initially requires very little expense of energy, choosing to resolutely favor either liberty or justice.

But Nature does not appear to exist in quiet states. Newton's Third Law notes that every action is balanced by an equal and opposite reaction. Nature manifests itself in innumerable arrays of tenuous states of dynamic equilibrium, each involved in a perpetual game of tug-of-war of reciprocal forces. Perhaps liberty and justice should be perceived as similar to such forces.

It is reciprocal forces that keep a tiny electron cloud close, yet not too close, to its atomic nucleus. Similarly, at the opposite end of the scale of our universe, it is the balance of the opposing forces of nuclear fusion and gravity that temporarily hold a massive star together in an uneasy state – a stand-off between the perilous possibilities of being drawn into a black hole, or blasted into space in a supernova explosion.

It is the very presence of opposing forces that allow both the atom and the star to exist, each wondrously engaged in a sinuous dance of pushing and pulling, of give and take.

Between these wide margins of our existence resides an infinity of interrelated forces that are likewise at once contradictory and complementary; such as darkness and light, heat and cold, reason and emotion – and perhaps even liberty and justice. And it is within this incredible collection of balanced and interconnected opposing forces that we experience our human condition.

Note that the first word of "cognitive dissonance" implies a state of thinking, rather than a default to simpler and potentially more dangerous emotional responses. It is imperative that we *embrace* the human condition of cognitive dissonance; i.e., the process of simultaneously holding conflicting beliefs, particularly as it relates to competing ideals that are each meritorious in their own right – such as liberty and justice. The ability to contemplate and reconcile opposing forces is a vital part of what creates the optimal human experience.

As noted, if a person wishes to diminish the anxiety that they experience from holding conflicting beliefs or desires (the feeling of cognitive dissonance), they must either refute, ignore, or *alter* one or both of the dissonant factors. Some people choose to refute or ignore, seeking a quiet state; because, as is often said, ignorance is bliss. And sometimes it truly is…up until it isn't.

To ignore or refute a competing belief is often to focus excessively on self and immediacy – but this will only work for a short while. Over time, facts have a way of becoming too insurmountable for a logical person to ignore or refute. To find lasting resolution and happiness, one cannot effectively diminish their feelings of cognitive dissonance by forever refuting or ignoring one of the dissonant factors.

Instead, equilibrium is best attained by *altering* one or both of the opposing factors. In the case of liberty and justice, the dissonant factors are optimally modified by the act of *each entity yielding a part of itself to the other*. An individual must sacrifice a measure of their personal liberty (freedom) for the greater good; and the collective must bend the reed of justice (fairness) a bit, allowing for a measure of autonomy of the individual. It is a never-ending process of give and take.

Recall the familiar symbols of yin and yang, composed of two comma shaped entities, one black and one white, joined together in a tight embrace within a circle. Within the black entity is a small circle of white, and within the white entity is a small circle of black; signifying that each entity surrenders a part of itself to the other.

Yin and yang describe forces or entities that are in some ways opposite, yet also complementary to each other. The two come together to make a whole – such as male and female, black and white, warm and cool – without assigning any degree of judgment (good or bad) to one entity or the other.

The equally meritorious entities of liberty and justice can also be thought of this way, perhaps considered to coexist on the same side of a spinning coin (the other side of this coin represents subjugation and injustice). Like yin and yang, liberty and justice must each yield a portion of themselves to the other, if both are to fully thrive.

If we were to value only personal liberty, we might speed our cars down neighborhood streets at 100 mph, remaining unconcerned about the possible injustice of hitting a pedestrian. If we were to value only justice, we would never risk hurting any pedestrian at all, and we would always leave our cars at home. To find a reasonable resolution, we choose to drive, but to drive more slowly. We find a balance between liberty and justice – by giving up a small measure of each.

When examined closely, many major social issues often distill down to weighing the value of liberty against the value of justice – freedom vs. fairness.

It is imperative that humankind continuously engages in the uneasy dynamic equilibriums of Nature and Life, centered around the constantly moving target of achieving the greater good. It is worth the price of cognitive energy to simultaneously honor opposing yet complementary factions or ideals, each worthy in their own right, and each balancing the other.

We must make the effort to seek compromise. We must jump into the messy and complicated middle ground, where the forces of liberty and justice – freedom and fairness – must always each be honored.

There is no static exact center point between liberty and justice, rather a dynamic middle ground defined by continuous episodes of pushing and pulling, advance and retreat, debate and compromise.

Cultures change. Even logic changes, depending on prevailing circumstances. Sometimes the value of liberty must exceed that of justice, and sometimes it is the value of justice that must by favored over liberty. In the symbolism of yin and yang, the circle of color that is given one to the other is constantly changing in size, smaller to larger and back again, in a never-ending cycle.

And, finally, the expression of opposing forces (or opinions) must not be emotionally reduced to violent battles pitting good vs. evil, right vs. wrong. Just like the values of liberty and justice, opposing entities are often each commendable in their own right; each necessary to balance the other.

There is great beauty in a universe comprised of opposing yet complementary forces. With each revolution of Earth, nighttime stars fade into morning light, and daylight later yields back to evening darkness – Night and Day briefly fusing together in spectacular magenta brilliance. It is a glorious and colorful dalliance of give and take, of beginning and end, of dawn and dusk.

With hearts and minds open to valuing both liberty and justice, we can boldly enter the fray, attempting to find common ground regarding many issues that tend to divide us. On the pages to follow, some of humankind's many present challenges are evaluated – and middle-ground starting points for friendly discussion are suggested.

Capitalism and Socialism

As with many other issues or cultural constructs, when evaluating the relative merits of Socialism versus Capitalism, the most desirable economic and political systems can incorporate select elements of each ideal – recognizing the benefits of providing both personal liberty and collective justice to a nation's populace.

Requiring the art of compromise and collaboration, utilitarian agendas that benefit the masses must be balanced by principles that protect the sovereign rights of individual citizens.

Let's start with a couple of definitions:

Capitalism is defined as an *economic* and *political* system advocating that a country's trade and industry are controlled by private owners rather than by the state.

Socialism is defined as an *economic* and *political* system advocating that the means of production, distribution, and exchange should be owned or regulated by the community as a whole.

The Person/People/Planet triangular relationship can be a useful construct when considering these systems. Recall that this concept considers the individual, the collective, and the Earth itself as equal and inseparable; each entity linked to the others as an integrated whole.

Similarly, the *individual* liberty afforded by Capitalism, and the *collective* justice provided by Socialism, can balance each other; with each system equally reliant on a forever flourishing planet.

In a capitalist system, maximizing profit is typically the prime directive. In its most pure form, Capitalism follows some of the same rules as Darwinism, the overarching ecological construct within which survival of the fittest is the rule. In Nature, every creature must always pull its own weight; and the slow and weak do not survive. Capitalism somewhat mimics Nature, ranging from benevolent to brutal, depending on one's place in the food chain.

Capitalism is in part steeped in meritocracy, because effort and execution do indeed pay off substantially in this system. But luck plays a big part as well – even though many of us may not like to admit to this. Being born into a wealthy family, or even into an affluent country such as the US, offers a person a tremendous advantage.

It is easier to make money if we already have money, particularly if we are surrounded by other rich people living in a safe environment with a vibrant economy. There are many wealthy citizens who forget to acknowledge the good fortune of their birth circumstances. They were born on third base, but like to think they hit a triple.

That said, in principle, a capitalist system allows all citizens the opportunity to climb the pinnacle of financial success from humble beginnings; especially individuals who reside in free democracies. Many people in the US have started life with two strikes against them, yet they have rounded the bases through hard work and perseverance.

Let's now take a brief look at Socialism. In its most unadulterated form, Socialism has historically performed quite poorly. Even today, one needs to look no further than Venezuela to note the corruption, devastation, and despair created by a socialist government.

A lack of reward for personal achievement can often lead to an effort by the workforce that is mediocre at best. And the Marxist ideal that absolute Socialism can be used as a stepping stone to Communism must certainly be recognized.

In their purest forms, Capitalism and Socialism are each flawed. A completely free-market system may work very well when pricing luxury items such as large-screen televisions. However, charging whatever the market will bear is not an appropriate strategy when it comes to treating basic human illness and suffering. We are our brother's and sister's keepers after all – and elements of Socialism recognize that.

Of course, there are often negative consequences with extreme forms of almost anything, and that includes political and economic systems. A properly blended mix of Capitalism and Socialism can provide humankind the best of each system. A balanced hybrid approach offers a compelling middle-ground solution; working to help soften a few of the sharp edges of a capitalist system.

Some people may wish to name this blended type of political and economic structure "Compassionate Capitalism," whereas a comparable hybrid system has also been called "Third Way" by others.

It can be fairly argued that an ideal political and economic construct could generally favor a *predominantly* "capitalist" system, but then add select "socialist" values to make it even better. This includes accepting precepts of increased social justice and equality; while concurrently roundly rejecting other characteristic socialist principles – such as state ownership of industry, the abolition of capitalism, and non-democratic governance. This system already exists to some degree in the US.

In recent years, millions of "capitalists" have cashed "socialist" stimulus checks delivered to them by our government. And, millions of senior citizens happily accept Social Security bank deposits, as well as Medicare payments for their healthcare. Protected by public law enforcement officers, we drive on public roads and bridges as we travel to public parks, public libraries, and public universities – all elements of Socialism embedded in a predominantly capitalist system.

In addition, some die-hard wealthy "capitalists" are indeed the most culpable of all "socialists" – lobbying for preferential tax treatment and subsidies, declaring bankruptcies, privatizing gains while socializing losses, and often accepting taxpayer bailout money after convincing government leaders that their companies are too big to fail.

Many Northern European countries presently employ hybrid political and economic systems composed of elements of both Socialism and Capitalism (often called the Nordic Model). These nations tend to utilize a few more social programs than are presently offered in the US.

Finland, a predominantly capitalist country, is an example of one such hybrid model. There are billionaires who live in Finland, but not many. Finnish citizens pay higher taxes than their American counterparts, to be sure. However, they also enjoy free healthcare, subsidized childcare, generous vacation time and maternity leave, and free college tuition. Of note, Finland has been ranked the happiest country in the world the last eight years in a row. Other Scandinavian countries likewise rank high on happiness indices. Denmark, Finland, Norway, and Sweden are also ranked in the top eight least corrupt nations in the world by Transparency International (the US ranks 28th).

Presently, Northern European countries may generally reside further left on the political and social spectrum than many US citizens wish to be. However, even Nordic nations appear to be in little danger of becoming truly Socialist countries. And a possible slide into Communism would be more unlikely yet. Capitalism has served them well, and they know it.

Indeed, there is evidence that decades of Capitalism and its attendant strong work ethic is what helped to create the means for Scandinavian countries to have the robust economy and socialist-leaning safety net they enjoy today. Adding in widespread social services to a democratic predominantly capitalist system has worked quite well for them.

Nevertheless, as with every issue or concern, care must be taken, lest the pendulum swings too far. There are rumblings that cultural norms could be changing in Scandinavia, and that the idea of taking responsibility for one's own well-being might be starting to wane a bit. The challenge is of course to find the sweet spot – one where citizens in need are offered a hand up, but not necessarily a hand-out.

Although it is imperfect, Capitalism today appears to likely be the best foundation from which to build a stable economic and political system. Capitalism can perhaps be thought of as similar to the main course of a fine meal, where side dishes of Socialism are essential accoutrements to enhance the dining experience.

It is certainly reasonable for citizens to wish to avoid a complete and pure form of Socialism. That model has not worked well. As former UK Prime Minister Margaret Thatcher once noted, "The problem with socialism is that you eventually run out of other people's money." Nevertheless, it is an unfounded fear to worry that to crack the "socialism" door open a bit means it will soon be flung wide open.

In a scenario that some "conservative" individuals may fear, the US economic and political system could possibly morph into something like that of Scandinavia. That is indeed possible, although not necessarily probable. And, it would be very unlikely that our country would migrate into true Socialism, even if we did indeed follow many aspects of the Nordic model.

What would be more likely is that extremely wealthy US citizens would pay significantly more taxes, while most others would pay just a modest amount more – however, each would also qualify for many additional services. Overall, we would perhaps end up somewhere between the Nordic model and where we are now in the US.

As with the citizens of Finland, it is quite possible that the majority of US citizens might be a little happier with a few more social services. And *every* person, rich or poor, would benefit from the societal stability associated with a decrease in the wealth gap, better and more equitable health outcomes, and the provision of equal education opportunities.

Some far-left individuals appear to want more than that. Some even seem to demonstrate disdain for all wealthy people as a matter of course – conveniently forgetting about the multitudes of affluent philanthropists, past and present, who have greatly reduced misery on our planet. Pushing hard and fast toward pure Socialism, some far-left outliers appear to demand equality of *outcome* for all, instead of equality of *opportunity*.

By doing so, ultra-left individuals risk a ferocious political backlash – one in which opposing conservative party members may retreat into equally extreme and distant fortresses; far away from the middle, venturing into the encampments of far-right individuals. Similar to many center-focused citizens, these fringe-right people may indeed favor an *economic* system of Capitalism; however, they also often tightly embrace radical and violent *political* agendas as well.

We see evidence of this today throughout the world. Many far-right agendas stretch beyond emblematic conservative ideals; some even encouraging the emergence of authoritarian-type leaders who preach a message of intolerance, exclusivity, and violence.

Danger lurks at the margins. Middle-ground compromises are essential – particularly when instituting economic and political systems.

A Note Regarding Human "Rights"

The universe does not award inherent "rights" to any living creature. An Alaskan salmon offers no rights to its herring prey, nor does it receive any from the grizzly bear before it, too, is devoured. A hawk is not born with the right to have a nest to live in, a mouse to eat each day, or its injuries looked after. From the perspective of the universe, no creature is born unto our Earth with any guaranteed rights at all. And, throughout its existence, nothing is ever owed to any living form.

The universe makes no promise of fairness. The gift we are given is but a chance at Life itself – the incredible opportunity to forge one's path in a beautiful and terrifying world of creative destruction, where both promise and peril await beyond each turn.

We are simply given the chance to play in the grand game; to participate in this fantastic adventure – which is perhaps a greater gift than any guarantee of fairness.

As with any creature of Earth, humans have no inherent universal "right" to food, housing, or health care. When we are born, the universe does not owe us anything. The "rights" granted to (and by) human individuals are not the result of a divine cosmic obligation, rather a wise and benevolent gift given *from* ourselves *to* ourselves; bestowed in an attempt to institute a degree of fairness in an existence where none was ever promised.

The only "rights" that humans have are those deliberated upon and conferred by an assembly of other humans. These rights may be based on religious ideology, such as the right to "Life, Liberty, and the pursuit of Happiness" granted to Americans by our Constitutional forefathers, who believed such rights to be endowed to us by our Creator.

These rights may also be crafted today by other intelligent people, those who keenly understand that establishing rights for the individual will benefit the collective. Rights for humans are also often established by compassionate fellow citizens; kind souls who possess an innate desire to allay suffering in the world.

Human rights are simply a set of ideals and aspirations created *for* humans, *by* humans. Nevertheless, they are an essential element in humankind's successful journey to Sustainable Global Happiness.

But these rights also come with a set of rules. A wolfpack grants all its members the right to a portion of the catch, but the pack leader also requires that each wolf takes part in the hunt. If a human populace wishes to fully thrive, it must similarly grant certain rights to all its members – such as the right to safe shelter, nutritious food, and appropriate health care – but it must likewise require that its members all pitch in, to the best of their capabilities.

In the US, most jobs are based on a 40-hour full-time work week. It is therefore reasonable to expect all able adults to work full-time, if that is what is necessary to cover their own needs, or the needs of their family. However, it is also reasonable to guarantee any adult who is working full-time, at any job, at least enough financial compensation to pay for adequate shelter, nutritious food, appropriate healthcare, and childcare.

In essence, it is in the best interest of every nation to offer each of its citizens a livable wage for an honest day's work.

Presently, in the US in 2026, fulfilling that ideal would require a federal minimum wage of at least $20/hour or more, depending on locale. Exemptions for paying lower wages could be made in some circumstances, such as for businesses that hire trainees or interns, and those that employ students and dependents under 18 years of age.

There are some individuals who oppose increasing the minimum wage to a livable level. Many of these people seem to ascribe to the capitalist market certain qualities that it does not deserve, almost believing it to be a sort of supernatural force that fairly and efficiently dispenses financial justice – culling the weak from the strong, and single-handedly creating the best of all societies. It makes for a nice, tidy story.

But life is not always nice and tidy. Like a prairie wildfire, market forces are very real and powerful, and they indeed often provide a benefit to an environment. But, left uncontrolled, they also have the potential to unleash untold misery.

Although Capitalism without oversight may work out well for some, it simply does not work out well for most. Pure Capitalism is like playing a US football game without pads, rules, or referees – a competition where more players may end up in the hospital than on the field. And those remaining in the game are sometimes there for reasons involving luck as much as skill.

A livable minimum wage would help decrease our nation's wealth disparities, the presence of which usually foments discord in any population. Many people who oppose a livable minimum wage appear to have forgotten what it is like to work in the trenches – or perhaps they have never experienced them.

I am personally familiar with the trenches. In years past, I labored in many different types of jobs, some of which were quite difficult and low-paying. As a young boy, I would ride a bus with my brother to local farms where we were hired to pick strawberries, and later beans, in the lush summer fields of Oregon's Willamette Valley.

As an older teenager, I bussed tables and washed dishes at a steakhouse restaurant. I cleaned golf clubs and picked up driving range balls at a country club. I loaded baggage at the local airport. I bucked hay. I stacked blocks of ice into trucks that were not tall enough to stand completely upright in. I spent a very short time working evenings as a janitor.

In several summers between college and medical school terms, I labored in various sawmills, pulling heavy boards of lumber of both small and large dimensions off conveyer chains; stacking them in loads to be delivered to lumber yards where they would be sold to help build our nation.

Each of my jobs had a certain dignity about them, and each served to help advance humankind in its own way. It is imperative that individuals who work similar jobs today be paid a livable wage, allowing them their own opportunity to thrive.

A livable minimum wage would also help to improve our nation's homelessness problem. It is not a demonstration of compassion to allow unhoused individuals to live in makeshift shelters without sanitation; constantly exposed to extreme weather, violence, alcohol, and drugs. Many of these people also suffer from inadequately treated addiction and/or mental health issues.

One possible solution to help with the homelessness problem could look something like this:

Every unhoused individual would become eligible to receive subsidized public housing, such as in apartment complexes or tiny-home communities. Any able person who could not find employment would be enrolled in a federal jobs program that paid a livable wage (similar to the Civilian Conservation Corps created by US President Franklin D. Roosevelt). Work would include activities such as structure building and trail maintenance in local and national parks, wildfire prevention, tree planting, roadside beautification, urban and rural farming, and other community-focused endeavors.

Performing these essential jobs for society would help participants learn new job skills, as well as instill in them a sense of purpose and confidence. A livable wage would also allow program members to help pay for their housing and medical care costs.

Addiction counseling/treatment and outpatient mental health services would be readily available at no cost. Inpatient facilities would be provided for persons unable to care for themselves, or who are a threat to others. Subsidized public transportation and childcare would also be readily accessible to program participants.

The universe offers no inherent "rights" to any person. However, there is room in the political and economic systems of noble societies to offer every citizen the opportunity for Life, Liberty, and the Pursuit of Happiness. Sometimes that may take a helping hand.

Diversity

"So, let us not be blind to our differences – but let us also direct attention to our common interests and to the means by which those differences can be resolved. And if we cannot end now our differences, at least we can help make the world safe for diversity. For, in the final analysis, our most basic common link is that we all inhabit this small planet. We all breathe the same air. We all cherish our children's future. And we are all mortal."

                                             –John F. Kennedy

My hope is that Earth's increasingly intermingled populations of diverse peoples and cultures will all be met with warm acceptance; adding richness to our human experience, and further expanding our shared identity. My hope is for humankind to use the power of our differences to build a better world, and to never let our differences keep us apart.

If we were tasked to construct a magnificent building, we would be wise to enlist the services of a varied array of architects, engineers, carpenters, and crafts-persons to help us – bringing together the visions and skills of a diverse group of artisans to create a unified masterpiece. And, so it is with building a better world.

Diversity provides portals from which to see the world anew. To gain a clear vision of the destination of Sustainable Global Happiness, it is best to view it through the lenses of many different individuals and cultures. This vision is most optimized if we first clear our own lenses of any biases that constrain our field of view – opacities based on fear, selfishness, or unawareness that can hinder our journey to a peaceful, just, and flourishing planet.

Unconscious Bias

None of us are born with any inherent biases regarding another person's nationality, race, religion, gender, sexual orientation, age, disability, occupation, income level, physical appearance, or any other difference. Yet, by the time we are adults, we often harbor biases regarding characteristics we note in others.

Some of our biases are at a conscious surface level, and we can often easily recognize them in ourselves. Other biases are at a sub-conscious (unconscious) level; and we are often unaware of their presence.

We often use our unconscious biases to size people up very quickly – although quite often not very accurately – and we do so by using cognitive shortcuts (heuristics) derived from our past experiences. The use of rapid appraisals such as these may have provided our ancestors a genetic advantage, as quickly identifying a person as "other" may have prevented potential harm from a warring tribal enemy.

Today, our biases are of course not only constructed from direct personal experience, but also from societal influences – our families, friends, teachers, and the media. These preconceptions are created from a composite of our interactions (real or virtual) with individuals who may be different than us. The cultural stereotypes we have been repetitively exposed to can easily become imbedded within our subconscious minds.

Of course, no person is immune to unconscious bias. People with lighter skin color may harbor unconscious biases against those of darker shades of color. Likewise, people with darker skin color may hold similar biases against those whose color is unlike their own (this is not to imply moral symmetry regarding events that may have helped create these biases). It is the same for rich people and poor people, "liberals" and "conservatives," religious and non-religious individuals, and any other people or groups of people who are different from one another. We often subconsciously judge every person we meet.

Fortunately, many of our conscious and unconscious biases can be transformed by thoughtful consideration of accurate information. For example, it is possible that some conservative-leaning people may alter their biases after learning that immigrants to the United States are on average no more likely to commit crimes than are native-born citizens. And the biases of some liberal-leaning people may perhaps start to change upon learning that individuals in the top one-half income bracket already pay 97% of all US federal income taxes.

Humans often prefer to live in echo chambers, getting our stories from friends and media outlets that support our point of view, often omitting from the narrative items that might challenge the perspectives we hold so dear.

Celebrating our Unique Cultures Together

It appears to be in our genetic makeup to be social, and many of us therefore find comfort in finding groups in which to belong. However, as with nearly everything else, there is often trouble at the margins. Focusing exclusively on one's own particular cultural or ideological group can lead to a tribalistic mentality; one in which those who are considered different are often feared or reviled.

Conversely, if we smooth out all the bumps in human societies, becoming *too* homogeneous of a population, we miss out on many of the advantages that diversity can bring.

It is imperative to find the sweet spot of convergence, the place where people can maintain the individual culture and traditions of their niche group, but also benefit from interacting with every other group of humanity.

We should enjoy our own unique communities, certainly, but it is also essential that we frequently associate with people whose backgrounds are different than our own. Widening our circles gives us the opportunity to expand our happiness and social repertoire; enjoying and learning about other cultures as we each share our different stories, values, traditions, food, music, and art.

Of course, embracing diversity not only exposes us to differences in background, but to differences of perspective as well – and to opinions that we might not share. That said, respectful disagreement and discussion can certainly be a positive experience, as it often leads to improved outcomes. When we hear or read about a new point of view, it often requires us to better examine our own position. It may also enlighten us to facts we have not yet considered.

Differences need not evolve into arguments as a matter of course; rather they can provide talking points for calm discussion – with the ultimate goal of advancing the ideal of Sustainable Global Happiness. It is quite possible for two parties to respectfully (perhaps even cheerfully) disagree. Each person should aspire to listen twice as much as they speak – knowing that we learn more by listening to others than by listening to ourselves.

We cannot bridge our great divides if we forever remain on our own side of the river. We can consider crossing a few bridges, to engage with people who are different than us. We can extend a friendly countenance to every person we meet; listening to their stories, and imagining what it is like to walk in their shoes.

It starts with a smile and a "hello."

The Responsibility of the Collective

Our individual and collective lives parallel Nature in many ways. In a river, the water that passes by today is not the same water as that of yesterday or tomorrow. But a river is not just the water itself, it is also the living forms within it, and the riverbed over which it flows. The flowing water of countless previous years carved channels through sediment and rock; creating eddies, rapids, and pools that are the essence of the river today.

Although yesterday's water is replaced by today's water, there remains a continuous strand of connectivity that brings the river's past, present, and future together as one living entity. And, so it is with humans – and with groups of humans.

Throughout our existence, nearly all the cells of our bodies come and go, being continuously replaced by newer versions. Yet we are still the same person. The connective strand of consciousness remains intact, much like the essence of a river from one year to the next.

Likewise, in the US, each of our lives our intimately connected to the lives of our predecessors and descendants; each of us an integral part of a living and constantly changing body of citizens, flowing through a shared existence for nearly 250 years.

Citizens of all nations are often bestowed many advantages from previous and present generations – a beneficial strand of connectivity most of us gladly accept. However, we often take this privilege for granted, forgetting that we may have been bequeathed a birthright that we ourselves never had to personally earn. We tend to believe that our individual successes are mostly due to our own cleverness and hard work; sometimes failing to fully appreciate the groundwork built by others before us.

Our nation's past, present, and future victories are indeed victories for us all. But *its* failures are also *our* failures, and all of its past is our past as well. We must take the bad with the good, as the garment of our nation's history is tightly interwoven with each. As such, we must today help remediate any errors that our predecessors may have made.

We appropriately recoil when we think of the terror and pain inflicted upon the approximately 4,000 Black men and women who were lynched in our country, many of whom were brutally tortured before being killed. In the US, there are still Black citizens alive today whose parents or grandparents lived in fear of a similar fate – and who themselves are justifiably worried that physical harm could also come to them, simply because of the color of their skin.

It will of course take time for continual healing to take place, as racial injustice still exists in our nation. In many regions, people of darker skin color still often face inequality in areas such as the criminal justice system, health care access/treatment, and voting access.

We are similarly stunned by the history of violent conquest of

North American indigenous populations and their land by early European settlers. The broken promises, unsigned treaties, and deaths of not only native warriors, but women and children as well, leaves an indelible stain on the legacy of the US.

Some people may note that slavery happened not just in the US, but all over the world, for many thousands of years. That is true. Some also may note that, throughout history, countless other nations have also vanquished indigenous populations and stolen their lands. That is also true. But it does not make these things right. We must not make excuses for our past. "Whataboutism" does not exonerate criminal behavior. We are better than that.

It is imperative that our schoolchildren learn all of the stories of our nation's history. It is not unpatriotic to tell a child the whole truth. Telling the truth is certainly not intended to make any of today's children feel personally guilty about themselves or our nation's past. No, not at all. Rather it is intended to engender an accurate understanding of humankind's past and present actions and biases, and to encourage a mindset of shared responsibility.

The United States certainly has countless noble and courageous chapters to be proud of, and it truly is an amazing nation. But we have also collectively committed egregious crimes along the way – and these injustices must be fully acknowledged and remedied.

In the end, when children are told the truth, they will love their country even more, not less. They may be astonished and saddened when learning of atrocities committed by people who are now long gone, but they can also be honored to be part of a new generation that thinks and acts differently; ready and willing to help remediate the actions of compatriots they likely never knew.

When these children are older, they will learn that every person, citizenry, and government has made mistakes – but you can only trust those that admit to and set right their errors.

Acknowledge, Remediate, and Advance

There will always be some individuals who choose to reside at the margins, no matter what the issue happens to be. Regarding diversity concerns, at one far edge reside a few outliers who appear to seek equality of *outcome* for all, rather than equality of *opportunity*.

At the opposite edge there are also some outliers; those who deny or make light of social injustices such as intolerance, discrimination, or extreme income disparities. Some of these people even demonstrate malicious speech and actions, appearing to truly lack empathy. Others seem to simply lack awareness of the true scope of the challenges, not realizing we have yet to achieve equality of opportunity for all.

And then there are the majority who reside in the middle. These citizens indeed recognize their nation's past, both good and bad, and have learned from it. They know of the present and persistent oppression leveled against diverse populations – yet they know, too, of the conscientious efforts of many individuals and coalitions tirelessly working to wipe it out. They understand that people of all forms of diversity are equally capable of greatness. They attempt to assess intolerance and discrimination with equanimity; focusing on apologies, forgiveness, remediation, and moving forward. They also wish to address the problem at the source cause; curing the disease, once and for all, rather than forever treating the symptoms.

It may take time, perhaps another generation, for wounds to further mend, and for remediation and forgiveness to take place. The injuries will heal, even though some scars will remain.

There can be some value in a scar – a remembrance of a past that must not be forgotten. Such past reminders are necessary; lest history does what it tends to do, which is to repeat itself. To *forgive* is indeed noble and right; but to *forget* is illogical – and sometimes dangerous.

Most people recognize that individuals of all colors and cultures are equally capable on a level playing field. However, the field is still not yet fully level, and the legacy-effects of racism, subjugation, and related poverty can be difficult to escape. We must eliminate persistent racism and other inequities that still exist today, and we must set right previous aggressions and unfairness. How best to do this?

Fighting Discrimination with Discrimination?

Many individuals rightly speak out against the many injustices that diverse minority populations endure because of their differences. Yet, perhaps somewhat incongruously, many of us also support exclusive advantages for these same groups – also because of their differences.

Some of these special advantages may include favorable treatment for individuals of diverse background, such as using quotas for job hiring or admission to college. To be clear, some systems of favoritism for diversity were, and are, a *short-term* necessity – because of the severe acuity of the problems of social injustice. However, they are not effective *long-term* solutions to the problem of inequality. As an example, regarding job-hiring or admission into educational institutions, it must be acknowledged that one person's gain is often counterbalanced by another person's loss.

Quotas and other forms of favoritism based on diversity often attempt to make up for a prior injustice by incurring a present injustice. However, it can perhaps be fairly argued that the best way to stop discrimination is to simply stop discriminating. Ideally, barriers should never be put in place for *any* person because of their heritage, age, gender, skin color, etc. – even if that person happens to be a wealthy male trying to gain admission to a prestigious university. Like a make-up call by a basketball referee, compounding one bad call by making another is not an enduring way to institute fairness.

Prejudice is prejudice. Fighting yesterday's prejudice with even more prejudice today cannot forever advance the ideals of social justice. One cannot continue to counter racism with more racism, or any social injustice with more social injustice. At their core, quota systems do indeed treat past injustices with present injustices, because for every person who is moved to the front of the line, there is perhaps an equally talented person who is moved to the back.

Nevertheless, in some areas, versions of favoritism are still a necessary band-aid fix – as it may take another generation to stanch the bleeding from intergenerational effects of intolerance and injustice. That said, while treating the *symptoms* of social injustice, we must simultaneously identify and resolve the root *cause*.

It can perhaps be fairly argued that the foremost cause of social injustice is **our failure to care about others as much as ourselves** – despite spiritual or political proclamations to the contrary. This failing of the social contract manifests in many ways – such as discrimination, inequitable distribution of public resources, and destruction of the environment (which disproportionately impacts marginalized and future human populations). Indeed, this moral shortcoming is present in nearly every type of injustice that humanity inflicts upon itself.

As such, all nations must make relentless efforts at great messaging – educating its students and citizens about the values of compassion, civic virtue, and intergenerational equity.

Nations must then *act* on these noble ideals; e.g., by providing equal opportunities for education and employment, and providing equal infrastructure and core public resources to *all* communities. Until that happens, favoritism based on diversity may continue to be an essential treatment. Instituting fairness is never perfect.

An Upstream Solution

Once again, as Albert Einstein said, "You can never solve a problem on the same level it was created." In that light, we cannot forever continue to treat past injustices with present injustices. Quota systems represent a short-term low-level solution that treats only the *symptoms* of the problem, rather than the *cause* of the problem.

A higher-level solution to the inequality problem is to go to the source, remediating past and present injustices by instituting upstream changes; creating *equality of opportunity* in every neighborhood.

Inequality must be confronted at its origin; curing the disease once and for all, rather than forever treating the symptoms. Efforts must be focused on the source of the problem, much of which is due to the unequal distribution of public resources to communities as a whole.

In a strategy of upstream remediation, the goal is to create a system whereby every runner begins from a fair starting line – a place from which success is achieved as a result of personal effort, rather than from birthright advantages.

To achieve this, **the poorest of neighborhoods must absolutely be equipped with public amenities equal to those of the richest of neighborhoods** – with the same access to education, scholarships, and technology. Although not a panacea, this is one core solution to the problem of inequality. Federal financial resources must go toward building excellent schools, community centers, parks, and libraries in *every* neighborhood, and to making job training uniformly available.

To help make part of this happen, methods of primary and secondary school funding could move toward a more centralized federal source, and away from local property taxes – the current system in which citizens residing in wealthier neighborhoods help pay for nicer schools and amenities for their children (NPR reports that school funding in the US presently varies between states but, on average, about 45% comes from local sources, 45% from individual states, and only 10% from the federal government).

Cooperative federalism is a difficult balancing act – weighing federal government rights against states' rights, i.e., honoring the supremacy clause of the US Constitution (wherein federal law supersedes state law) while also honoring the Tenth Amendment, which grants state control over issues not covered in the Constitution. States are often reluctant to relinquish control in any matter; however, a unified national response regarding equality of education infrastructure is imperative. All states would benefit from increased federal funding – providing equal learning opportunities for *all* our nation's children.

Great schools are, of course, at the heart of every great community.

Reparations

In 1946, the US government awarded approximately $1.3 billion to 176 Native American tribes and bands in reparations for centuries of conquest, averaging about $1,000 per tribal member. There have since been other scattered payments made to various tribes – to redress recent injustices regarding the use of natural resources on tribal lands.

In 1988, surviving Japanese-Americans interned in WWII received cash payment reparations, with about 80,000 individuals each receiving $20,000, for a total of $1.6 billion.

In contrast, to date, the only reparations paid to Black citizens by the US federal government was a $10 million payout distributed to the survivors and heirs of those who died in the Tuskegee Experiment, a forty-year study (1932-1972) of nearly 400 Black men conducted by the US Public Health Service to determine the effects of untreated syphilis. Enrollees in the study were not informed of their disease, even though an effective treatment was available in 1947.

There have been no federal reparations to compensate Black citizens for the legacy effects of slavery and Jim Crow laws, although some state and local governments have begun reparation efforts.

The US is currently the world's leading economic powerhouse, a fact largely due to the strength of its foundation. Created under the guidance of founding fathers, the US was physically built, in considerable part, by hundreds of years of backbreaking free labor provided by millions of Black slaves. These individuals are of course now long gone, and we can no longer ask their forgiveness, or offer personal recompense. But we do have the opportunity to reverse the untoward *legacy effects* our nation's actions had on their descendants.

Today, many US citizens do indeed acknowledge past injustices; yet some also argue that they are first-generation Americans, or that their ancestors arrived after slavery was abolished, and they therefore bear no responsibility for the actions of citizens who came before them.

However, just like buying into an existing business, all US citizens not only become part-owners of our nation's assets, they also absorb responsibility for all its debts and other liabilities as well. For instance, a first-generation US citizen cannot refuse to pay taxes to help pay down our national debt, even if they played no part in creating it.

As equal citizens, we must all take the bad with the good. As noted, our nation's past, present, and future victories are indeed our victories. But its failures are also our failures, and all of its past is our past as well. Reparations are therefore indeed necessary – and the obligation of all.

But how do we try to make good on our debts? At least presently, perhaps the best start is to make reparations *collectively*, upstream at the source – providing funding for beautiful state-of-the-art public schools, community centers, libraries, and parks in every neighborhood and indigenous population community. Of note, the allocation and design of these amenities must be chiefly determined by local community stakeholders.

Without question, the poorest of US neighborhoods deserve public amenities equal to those of the richest of neighborhoods. Yes, this will be a tremendous undertaking, involving a massive transfer of wealth, but it will be a *communal* wealth transfer of necessary restitution. It will also be a very sensible investment in the future of the United States.

Reparations to compensate for Black slavery – or any form of prior or persistent oppression to any group – can never completely repay our nation's debt regarding the social injustices incurred. Nevertheless, providing equitable community infrastructure is certainly a great start.

Words Matter

There are experts on diversity who do not like the use of the term "color-blind," often because they believe it does not acknowledge the difficulties that a person of color may have to overcome. They believe that a person who says they are blind to another individual's skin color, or perhaps other source of diversity, lacks awareness. Although that assertion could certainly be true, it may not always be completely fair.

Presently, with the exception of very young children, it is unlikely that humans can truly be blind to skin color, because we are all immersed in a society that has learned to elevate differences over similarities. For a person to be truly "color-blind" would require that citizens, of all colors, are always treated equally – which is certainly more an aspirational goal for humankind's future than a reality today.

That said, perhaps some people *attempt* to be "blind" – but only in regard to not seeing differences in skin color, or any other physical characteristic, as being related to a person's worth or ability. They truly wish for every person to be treated the same. They prefer to emphasize similarities in people, and they enjoy meeting others who are different than themselves, possibly in large part because they are personally enriched by it.

Perhaps unexpectedly, if humankind chooses to continuously focus on varying lighter or darker shades of skin color, it could be that we are inadvertently and insidiously validating its importance – breathing life into dying embers of thought processes that judge and define people by their visual appearance rather than by their character.

Perhaps many people who wish to be "color-blind" are not naïve, or trying to be offensive. Rather, they simply aspire to "see" others as a montage of their spirit, heart, and actions – while still acknowledging the severe injustices that many people face today, simply because of the color of their skin or other source of diversity. They do not wish to be blind to the reality of racism, intolerance, and discrimination. Perhaps they have just grown weary of the human tendency to categorize and evaluate people by their outward appearance; whether it is by their hairstyle, body shape or size, the clothes they wear – or the color of their skin.

Nevertheless, in the end, it is certainly best practice to abandon the term "color-blind," as it can imply different things to different people; causing disharmony in an area where there is already plenty.

Describing oneself as *"egalitarian"* is a better term. This word recognizes the unique challenges of people of color; as well as those faced by *all* diverse populations. An "egalitarian" is a person who knows that everyone is different – but sees all people as equal.

Another possible source of cultural disharmony is the use of the phrase "systemic racism." Systemic racism truly exists in the US and globally – there is no doubt about that. Indeed, there are still many individuals, scattered throughout America and the world, who treat people differently based on their race or ethnicity.

However, although racism is truly "systemic," because racist individuals are *widely* distributed, it is unknown how *densely* distributed they are. Determining that density is a nearly impossible task.

Also, the definition of *densely* distributed is quite subjective. For instance, hypothetically, if one percent of the world population were racist, some people might find that number to be encouraging – while others might point out that this would still represent nearly 80 million racist people across the globe.

Systemic racism is also sometimes called "institutional" racism, meaning that discrimination is imbedded in the laws, regulations, and culture of a society or organization. This includes discrimination in public and private places of employment, health care settings, education opportunities, and criminal justice systems.

Describing racism as "systemic" or "institutional" can be somewhat problematic, however, because some institutions in the above listed sectors perform far better or worse than others regarding equality, and there is sometimes also wide variability between individual states.

To some people, these terms might infer that racism is still *uniformly* manifest in most or all institutions or systems. These phrases may therefore possibly have the potential to underestimate or invalidate much of the hard work and accomplishments regarding diversity and equality that have been made so far.

Although there certainly remain countless racist people working in US institutions, there are also many citizens who can find no evidence of discrimination in their particular workplace at all; and especially not in the laws and regulations of their institution or company. In fact, they may daily witness government officials, corporate management, or fellow employees whole-heartedly encouraging diversity; via friendship, or in the hiring of minorities for key leadership positions.

Systemic and institutional racism absolutely still exist in our nation. However, these are imprecise terms and, as such, may have the potential to make them polarizing. It is perhaps better to adopt the phrase "*persistent* racism."

The bottom line is this: Persistent racism exists in the US and elsewhere today – and it remains a very significant challenge that humankind must relentlessly strive to entirely overcome.

This discussion of the semantics of intolerance and discrimination will be completed by evaluating one more term that has become politicized, and that is the word "woke." The cultural term "woke" was derived from the word *awake*; meaning to become more awakened and aware of injustice – which is of course a desirable attribute.

That said, this term (or its inferences) has been hijacked by people on each end of the political spectrum. On the "right," the word "woke" is used by some as a blanket derogatory label for progressive-leaning individuals. Here, it is often intended to demonize anyone who dares challenge the status quo, or who will not unfailingly lionize the US – even if some of its collective actions were, or sometimes are, perhaps more harmful than heroic.

Likewise, the idea of *appearing* "woke" is also sometimes used for tactical advantage by individuals or entities on the "left." Perhaps at times disingenuously, many companies and individuals publicly highlight their progressive virtue and abiding concern for the planet and all humanity. Of course, some entities and individuals truly do hold noble ideals, which they follow up with very commendable actions. For others, appearing "woke" could simply be a public relations move, designed to help them sell more of their goods and services – or maybe even make themselves more readily re-electable.

In 2020, in many US cities, small but violent subsets of otherwise peaceful Black Lives Matter (BLM) protestors damaged the respectability of a very worthy cause. And some government officials failed to be fair but firm with protesters; sometimes failing to ensure that those who committed acts of violence were arrested.

How much better for government leaders to walk hand-in-hand with marchers through city streets, absolutely demanding equality for all, but likewise demanding respect for personal property and the safety of others. That would demonstrate real "wokeness" – a real awareness of the plight of others, but also a similar real awareness that violence and retaliation are not effective means of remediation.

The overarching aim of the BLM movement, that of racial equality, must absolutely always be fully embraced. The use of violence, in response to any form of social injustice, must always be condemned. Martin Luther King's courageous message of unrelenting peaceful protest is an essential guiding precept for *all* social justice movements.

Regarding refrains sometimes used in response to the BLM slogan, such as "All Lives Matter" or "Blue Lives Matter" – of course they do. No one is suggesting otherwise. Most police officers are good people; bravely willing to perform a very dangerous and often thankless job. The phrase "Black Lives Matter" does not infer that *other* lives do not matter, or that Black lives matter *more*. It just means that Black lives matter, *too*. It means that, just like everyone else, people with darker skin color deserve to be treated the same as all other citizens, that's all. Being awakened to this ideal is a very good thing.

In the end, it is best to abandon the term "woke." Being "aware" is a better term to use. Every citizen – left, right, or center – must maintain a constant *awareness* of intolerance and discrimination.

A Path Forward

We must certainly be aware of our differences, but we must focus even more on our similarities. We must acknowledge that every human being is suffering, at least to some degree, no matter how well they may hide it. Everyone wants to fit in and be accepted – a primal need embedded in our DNA.

We must attempt to see every person as an individual…who also happens to be part of a group…which also happens to be part of one great tribe of humanity. We must realize that our similarities are greater than our differences. Each of us must also know that, in some way, *every* human being has something they can teach us.

It is vitally important that all global citizens know the whole truth regarding their nation's history – not a redacted version. Exposing the truth may indeed risk re-opening old wounds, but it is a necessary process, nonetheless. *The truth shall set us free.*

It is also important that we faithfully acknowledge the efforts of countless individuals, past and present, of all cultures and skin colors, who have joined the fight against discriminatory practices.

We still have a tremendous amount of work to do, as learning how to capitalize on our differences for the greater good has indeed been a slow evolutionary process. But we are making significant headway, and we can take heart in that.

Today, there are many people of all colors, cultures, religions, and ideologies, happily working and playing together in their schools, churches, neighborhoods, and places of employment – enthusiastically embracing humankind's extraordinary diversity.

Our differences continue to make us stronger.

TEN

Population Awareness

I WAS RECENTLY speaking with a friend about the global human population of 8 billion people, and how that number probably exceeds the sustainable carrying capacity of our Earth – at least presently. The conversation made her feel uncomfortable, as addressing this problem can involve such deeply personal issues as individual liberty and family planning.

My friend's concerns are certainly valid. However, once again, personal liberties coexist with the framework of collective justice – and also with the limitations of our planet's finite resource base. Population numbers grow exponentially, and natural resources can concurrently become diminished in exponential fashion. A finite planet cannot maintain infinite population growth. In the end, it is simply a math problem.

Sure, technology will provide solutions that can help delay the inevitable. But, at some point, without limits to population numbers, our Earth would simply have too many people living on it. From a sustainability standpoint, it very likely already does.

So, how should we address this challenge? No one wants their government to tell them how many children they can have. But we also don't want our children and grandchildren destined to live on a hot, crowded, polluted, and dangerous planet.

Fortunately, we do not need any person or government agency to mandate the exact family size we are allowed to have. That policy was utilized in China and other locales – and it failed miserably.

What *does* work is to provide affordable access to contraceptive measures. The other key effort is to provide education – teaching citizens about the personal and collective benefits of smaller family sizes, and making sure that children (especially girls) can attend primary and secondary school. These strategies are presently working quite well in many places, and several countries have already markedly lowered their birth rates by utilizing these measures. In fact, over one-half of all nations presently have fertility rates less than 2.0, proving that it is indeed quite possible to lower global population numbers.

Nevertheless, there are still many areas (particularly in less economically-developed regions) that are currently experiencing a non-sustainable population explosion. We all live on one planet, and overpopulation *anywhere* can have global ramifications *everywhere*.

To be fair, Earth's problems related to overpopulation are certainly not confined to developing regions. Although citizens living in more economically-developed countries are presently more successful at lowering birth rates, on average they also utilize far more planetary resources and create far more pollution per person than do poorer regions. For example, on a per person basis, the US emits 3 times more CO_2 than the global average, and 30 times more than the citizens of Bangladesh. Environmental sustainability is closely related to both global population numbers *and* societal consumption patterns.

Population concerns could also likely soon be further compounded, as we are on the cusp of medical breakthroughs that could significantly increase human longevity. This could possibly mean even more people on the planet, all living longer and collectively polluting more – and all competing for dwindling resource supplies. Resource demand outpacing supply is a potential peril of overpopulation, particularly regarding its association with geopolitical instability and warfare.

A significant increase in global population would likely bring misery to the planet – via food and water insecurity, more pollution, climate change effects, and new pandemics related to human encroachment on animal habitat.

To be considered also is simply the human emotional toll of overcrowding – traffic jams, long lines in the marketplace, and just too many sweaty people sitting beside us at a sunny beach. Excessive population exacerbates nearly every challenge that humanity presently faces.

We run into a bit of a conundrum when attempting to satisfy humankind's opposing desires of simultaneously achieving both economic growth and planetary sustainability. The current paradigm of continuous economic growth and quest for power requires more people to provide greater production and more military might – not to mention more tax revenues. Many leaders justifiably wonder who will support future aging populations if birth rates decline.

In a continuous growth model, more young people are needed to provide economic stability – and to pay taxes that help support older citizens via programs such as Social Security. However, our youth will of course also eventually get old, necessitating even greater numbers of new young people to replace them, and so on – resulting in an unending upward spiral of population growth. At some point, there would simply be more people than the planet could support. By necessity, steady-state economic models will have to replace humankind's present growth-oriented models.

There is a difference between what our Earth can support today, and what it can continue to do so *indefinitely*. Even with our present population of 8 billion people, Earth is already on artificial life support.

Humankind's crop yields are presently often dependent on irrigation from aquifers, many of which are becoming depleted faster than they can be replenished. These yields are also unsustainably propped up by the use of massive amounts of nitrogen fertilizer and dangerous pesticides. Problems with the overuse of synthetic fertilizer include soil acidification and degradation, nitrous oxide greenhouse gas emissions, and oceanic dead zones from eutrophication. Regarding synthetic pesticides, just like a human body with a failing liver and kidneys, our planet is exceeding its detoxifying capacity.

Via technology, our Earth may be able to support a few billion more people than it does today – but possibly only for a very short time. Up to this point, **human population growth has not been successfully decoupled from increased environmental damage.** More growth has gone hand-in-hand with worsening planetary destruction. And, as noted, without a sustainable and healthy planet, nothing else is possible.

Overpopulation thus represents an existential risk to humanity. As such, it is critically important that humankind begins to plateau and then lower its population numbers. At least presently, a slow and measured decrease in global birth rates would benefit our planet and all its future inhabitants.

The Global Footprint Network estimates that humankind would require 1.75 Earths to maintain our current level of consumption. Therefore, at this point in time, a global population of approximately 5 billion inhabitants is perhaps a reasonable aspirational goal. This approximate number is derived by using simple math ratios: 1.75 Earths/8 billion people = 1 Earth/4.6 billion people.

A relatively new technology called Precision Fermentation could possibly improve this ratio to some degree, as its widespread use could potentially help sustainably provide food to greater numbers of people.

Precision Fermentation involves genetically programming microorganisms to produce complex organic molecules (such as proteins, fats, enzymes, vitamins, and flavoring agents) in large steel vats. The inputs needed are electricity and simple plant sugars.

If proteins can be produced safely, affordably, efficiently, and at scale in fermentation vats, there would likely be less need to utilize animals for meat, dairy, and egg products. This would improve animal welfare, and potentially free up millions of acres of agricultural land to more efficiently support the nutritional needs of a larger population – while also lowering greenhouse gas emissions, and increasing carbon sequestration via reforestation of some areas of farmland.

If Precision Fermentation does indeed fully achieve the claims of its supporters, there could possibly soon be an attendant significant disruption in global agricultural systems. Not all are in favor of this – as there are still potential problems to further investigate (e.g., materials use, waste disposal, microbe escape, taking focus off Agroecology, etc.)

Other future technologies and behavioral changes could help relatively decouple human population growth from environmental destruction – by creating a circular economy based on recycling and regeneration, rather than on extraction and waste.

The optimal number of humans on the planet – and within individual nations – will of course change over time. These numbers will depend on the relative mix of environmental destruction, planetary constraints, immigration, and the ascent of promising new technologies. However, at least presently, a global population of approximately 5 billion people remains a reasonable target to aspire to, as the timeline and character of possible future events are uncertain.

Keeping the Faith

The global landscape is constantly changing, and our thinking and actions must remain flexible and nimble enough to adapt with it.

As such, it is imperative that leaders of global faith institutions convene to reconsider policies regarding family planning, as many still strongly encourage large family sizes.

The intent here is not to challenge the general spiritual principles of any religion. Many faith-based organizations provide a tremendous amount of good to the world. However, it must also be recognized that the Earth does not have an unlimited carrying capacity – and this means we must all practice our belief systems within that constraint. Evolve or perish.

The edict "Be fruitful, and multiply" does not proclaim that humans should multiply their populations as quickly as possible, or to a limitless number. That could spell disaster for everyone.

Self-regulating Aspects of Nature

If humankind does not adjust its population numbers on its own, Nature may do it for us – an option that would quite likely involve a lot of pain. Our Earth often naturally keeps the population numbers of its species in check; via predation, food scarcity, and disease.

We see evidence of this today, even in human populations. A quick glance at the daily news informs us of numerous predatory skirmishes between nations, agricultural systems dependent on unsustainable inputs, and emerging infectious diseases and pandemics related to increased human encroachment into wildlife ecosystems.

The increase in global population has also been accompanied by higher levels of dangerous environmental toxins. As a suspected consequence of exposure to some of these chemicals, human male fertility has dropped significantly over the last fifty years – perhaps one of many warning indicators that something is drastically wrong in our environment.

Predictions Can Be Tricky

Many economists correctly point out that Thomas Malthus was wrong back in 1798, when he predicted that our Earth would be unable to provide for a significantly larger human population. Malthus' mistake was that he failed to recognize that future technological innovations would allow for far more food production than he could possibly imagine.

But before anyone tosses Malthus too far under the bus, they must remember one very important thing – and that is the devastating impact on the environment caused by large numbers of people. Sure, we are feeding, housing, and transporting 8 billion people – but we are severely stressing the planet to do it.

Thomas Malthus was wrong; but he was somewhat close to being right. He just didn't use the word *sustainably*. With business as usual, our Earth cannot *sustainably* support excessive numbers of people. Of note, even with humanity's current use of non-sustainable agricultural practices, nearly 1 billion global citizens are presently undernourished.

Humans are choosing "low-cost" and non-sustainable models today, and forgetting about the rapidly mounting external costs for the future. We are indeed creating more food and goods for less dollars; but we are simultaneously generating catastrophic weather events – while also polluting our oceans, atmosphere, and land masses. As such, we are killing the coral reefs, insect pollinators, and keystone creatures that support Earth's life-giving ecosystems. Without a sustainable and healthy planet, there can be no sustainable population.

GDP vs. the Environment

Presently, the world's 15 wealthiest countries have fertility rates lower than replacement levels – a trend some economists find quite worrisome. With waning population growth, these economists fret about a possible decrease in global productivity and GDP (Gross Domestic Product). They also envision a possible slowdown of innovation, and difficulties associated with funding greater numbers of pensioners with fewer citizens in the workforce.

There are indeed potential problems with too low of fertility rates, and a sweet-spot of optimal population should be aimed for. But there is asymmetry when comparing the potential problems of *under*-population with those of *over*-population; as the issues of the latter are much more profound and difficult to remedy.

It is certainly possible that population numbers could plummet too quickly in some regions. However, that potential concern is one with ready solutions. For instance, governments could offer tax advantages or direct payments to couples with larger family sizes if needed.

Moreover, when new technological advances come to fruition, global productivity could likely *increase* – even if population numbers were to significantly wane. As such, with more available time, money, and hope for the future, many couples might opt for larger families, even without the possible need for financial incentives to do so.

It is true that the consequences of lower global birth rates could possibly be economically significant; however, this would likely be a short-lived event. In contrast, the consequences of higher global birth rates would nearly assuredly be economically *and* environmentally profound and long-standing – at least if massive and rapid changes in human behavior and innovation are not soon realized. Presently, the trend of lowered fertility rates is much more cause for celebration than concern (of note, the global population is still increasing each year).

As mentioned, population growth has yet to decouple itself from worsening environmental destruction. This association is growing even more dangerous, as citizens of economically-developing nations are understandably choosing to live more like their wealthier neighbors – traveling more frequently, consuming more goods, and eating more animal products. If present societal behaviors persist, an increase in global population will quite likely be accompanied by an increase in environmental toxins, greenhouse gases, and other forms of pollution.

These events due to overpopulation would not only be costly in regards to humankind's health, happiness, and safety, but enormously costly in dollars as well. The resultant catastrophic weather events, destroyed fisheries, toxic waste cleanups, and illnesses of global citizens would incur massive financial costs to humanity – greatly exceeding any possible relative loss of GDP related to lower population numbers.

Concerns regarding the possible effects of lowered fertility rates on global productivity and GDP are not unfounded, at least at first glance. However, from a long-term economic standpoint, it must be remembered that the Earth is our primary source of wealth.

Real wealth originates from our planet's rich soils, lush forests, mineral resources, and clean water with abundant fisheries. These provide food for humanity, and lumber and other materials from which we build our homes and run our businesses. These resources also become vehicles for commerce; for which humans have developed *paper* wealth, to assist with investments and the buying and selling of goods. Paper wealth includes currencies, stocks, and bonds – however, these are simply proxies for resource-based *real* wealth.

It is imperative to realize that all wealth originates from our planet and its flourishing ecosystems. Our economic security and GDP – and humankind's entire existence – are wholly dependent on a sustainable and regenerative Earth, and the Sun that powers it.

When evaluating the importance of GDP, it is also essential that we extend our time frame to consider the economic concerns of *all* generations, present *and* future. If resources such as clean air, pure water, rich soils, lush forest lands, and mineral deposits are imperiled by pollution and scarcity due to overpopulation, there will likely be many nations willing to fight to obtain them. As one of the lesser consequences of war, global GDP tends to plummet during times of major conflict. **If there is no sustainable Earth, there will be no sustainable GDP – it is as simple as that.**

It is also fair to question whether a growing GDP should be the primary yardstick with which to measure humankind's success. For instance, as a way of moving beyond just GDP, the country of Bhutan utilizes a Gross National Happiness index.

This is not to say that GDP is unimportant. Although the wealth gap between the rich and poor continues to widen, rising global productivity has indeed lifted billions of people out of poverty – as all ships rise and fall with the sea. Nevertheless, to think that higher fertility rates always proportionately increase productivity would be a faulty assumption, otherwise highly-populated regions such as Sub-Saharan Africa would all have a very high GDP.

There are other potential concerns regarding lower birth rates – such as the impact of lowered population numbers on future global innovation, as well as the issue of funding retirement for pensioners.

Regarding innovation, some economists argue that we need higher fertility rates because young citizens are more innovative, and they will be the people who invent the most important new technologies.

Not everyone shares this opinion – in the US, the average age of founders of startups, and holders of new patents, is over 40 years of age. Even so, roughly one-half of our present global inhabitants are under 30 years of age, meaning there are now 4 billion young minds available to help humankind solve its future problems. That is a lot of brain power.

One can compare this number to the *total* global population at the time many great polymaths were alive; such as Leonardo da Vinci – total global population less than 0.5 billion; Isaac Newton – less than 1 billion; Albert Einstein – less than 2 billion. And, far different from today, these brilliant individuals lived at a time when the vast majority of the global populace was largely uneducated.

Innovation is of course immensely important. Indeed, nations that are the best innovators are set up to be the future global leaders. That said, the argument that humankind has yet to reach the critical population mass necessary to optimally innovate does not hold water. Our country, and our Earth, do not need greater numbers of humans to guide us. We just need our current inhabitants to be educated to the greatest degree possible.

The other stated concern, that of funding a growing number of pensioners via the labor of a relatively smaller workforce, is certainly a more difficult challenge. As noted, possible future increases in productivity from technological advances, and a resultant surge in relative financial prosperity, could help offset this problem. Still, this funding issue must be addressed now, as the future holds too many uncertainties. Current generations may therefore have to make some sacrifices – to help humankind regain its collective financial footing.

As such, in some locales, workers may need to retire later in life, perhaps accept some budget cuts to social services, and possibly pay higher taxes. Regional workforce shortages may also likely need to be managed with carefully regulated immigration.

Undoubtedly, these strategies will be a tough sell. Few politicians get elected by promising fewer benefits, increased taxes, and more immigration. Skillful messaging is indeed essential.

Humankind's Potential Lifespan

If we choose to advance our species wisely, we collectively have the potential to exist on our planet far into the future. Life on Earth may ultimately be limited only by the physical characteristics of our Sun – which scientists estimate is about halfway through its eight-billion-year lifecycle. Over the next few billion years, our Sun will slowly mature into a red giant of increasing brightness, eventually making our planet too hot to be inhabitable by humans.

Some scientists believe we have about one billion years left for our Earth to remain in the habitable zone, where liquid water remains stable on our planet. Of course, a remaining one-billion-year timeline for human life on our planet is certainly not a prediction, rather just a hopeful possibility – barring planetary bombardment by giant asteroids, a nuclear holocaust, virulent global pandemics, or other unforeseen events of the future.

Anthropologists note that modern humans (Homo sapiens) have been around for only about 300,000 years. If one *billion* years is perhaps the ultimate limit of humanity's remaining time on Earth, we could quite possibly be only in the very early stages of our prospective journey as a species.

The human race can perhaps gain encouragement and a glimpse of its potential collective lifespan from dragonflies. These majestic little creatures have been gracefully flitting over our planet for more than 350 million years – long enough to watch the dinosaurs come and go.

Changing Behaviors

Some people think that overpopulation is not a major problem for humankind, rather it is our excessive consumption that is the issue. Others believe it is neither overpopulation or overconsumption that matters most, suggesting we simply need to use Earth's resources more efficiently, decrease our pollution, and stop wasting so much food.

All great ideas, to be sure. However, unfortunately, these noble aspirations have yet to be realized. Humans often think more about self and immediacy, and less about others and the future – especially when we believe that our personal liberties or pocketbook might be threatened. Although we are progressing in this regard, our self-focused characteristics may not be vanishing anytime soon. Perhaps this is why clear messaging, good governance, and noble constitutions are so essential – to help protect us from ourselves.

Until we collectively choose to reverse our destructive behaviors, more people on the planet portends more trouble for the environment, and thus, for ourselves. And, even if humankind does lessen its environmental impact, there are still ultimate limits to growth on a finite planet.

Population Awareness is a critical aspect of achieving Sustainable Global Happiness. Efforts to improve global education and access to affordable contraception will result in population numbers optimized to maintain a flourishing and sustainable planet – creating a better life experience for all present and future Earth inhabitants.

ELEVEN

The Risks and Benefits of Rapidly Accelerating Technology

MY MOM WAS raised in a small sawmill-town in Washington state, and my dad's early childhood years were spent in a logging camp near the northern coast of California. They each had a father who worked tirelessly as a manual laborer, and a mother who worked equally diligently raising their respective families.

In the mornings, my parents would help bring wood kindling into their homes, which their mothers would use in wood-burning stoves to cook their family's daily meals. My father's house did not have running water, and going to the bathroom involved a trip to the outhouse.

Mom and Dad met in high school, fell in love, and became the best parents I could have ever hoped for; but that is a story for another day. They are in their late eighties now. It must seem to them like a long haul – all the places they have been, the meals prepared and eaten, and the tears and laughter shared throughout lives well-lived. But in geologic time, their rich and full lives have occurred in merely an instant, like the snap of a finger. And within this tiny sliver of time, they have witnessed many extraordinary changes.

My parents now of course have running-water and a modern oven in their house. If these do not seem like amazing advances, one might try turning off the power and water to their home for just a week.

My parents lived most of their lives in the 1900's – a century that spawned a green revolution in agriculture; the defeat of smallpox, polio, and Hitler; and the birth of space travel, nuclear weapons, television, smartphones, and the internet.

But, like the saying goes, "you ain't seen nothing yet." The exponential curve of progress continues to rise ever-steeper in this twenty-first century, and the future is coming at us faster and more furiously than ever before.

And it is literally a wild ride. We will soon be ferried about town in autonomous electric vehicles (EVs) – and probably flying air taxis, too, if we wish. Electric or hydrogen-powered bullet trains and hybrid-electric airplanes will also be available for longer trips.

There will be many more robot-assisted surgeries, increasingly personalized medicine, and new vaccines to help enhance our health and increase our longevity. Carbon-capturing machines will help lower global CO_2 levels; desalination plants and water purification systems will help provide potable water; and robots may be used to deliver a laser beam or electric charge to weeds, helping farmers to decrease their use of herbicides.

If we utilize our amazing technology with great care, the future does indeed hold great promise. However, if we do not remain ever vigilant, the future could also hold great peril.

It is imperative that humankind makes rules for our technological advances, as they offer not only tremendous benefit, but the possibility of massive societal disruption and suffering as well. Regarding any new technology, we must always ask ourselves: "Why?" and "For what worthy cause are we choosing this path?"

If the answer to that question is "To save or make money," that is usually not a good enough reason by itself. Costs matter, certainly. But it can be fairly argued that the prime directive of Life is not to make our personal and collective pocketbooks as fat as possible today, at the expense of everything else tomorrow. And, of course, short-term money savings can also often be associated with long-term money loss. It is imperative that we constantly expand our time horizons when considering the possible consequences of our present actions.

Sometimes, the enemy of good is better. Regarding technology, this sentiment is not to suggest that humankind should remain fearfully huddled in a foxhole. No, rather it is to realize that live ammunition is firing over our heads, and we must ask ourselves if the potential real estate gained by a new technology is worth the risk.

Precautionary principles must be utilized. Plans for the future must always recognize the possibility of low-probability events, particularly if such events could result in catastrophic consequences. Today, there are many technologies that come with both potential promise and potential harm – these include Genetic Engineering, Geo-engineering, Robotics, Artificial Intelligence, and Quantum Computing.

Like it or not, these genies are already out of their bottles, and they are not going back in – and they will continue to advance ever more.

As a world leader, it is imperative that the US always stays ahead of the curve; meaning that our government must relentlessly support science, technology, engineering, and mathematics (STEM). Humankind cannot collectively be asleep at the wheel, letting the future careen out of control wherever it will. We must optimistically go forward, to be sure, but we must pay close attention to where we are going, because potential danger lurks at every turn.

It is also critically important to understand that there are limits to which technology can help with our challenges. Scientific advances are of course absolutely necessary, but they are not a replacement for willpower and selflessness. Innovation must walk hand-in-hand with actions like reduce/reuse/recycle – and governments, businesses, and individuals must all do their part.

My parent's generation experienced many miraculous breakthroughs that greatly improved human lives. But they also lived through the era of WWII, and numerous other global wars and atrocities as well. They have seen science and technology used to build weapons of mass destruction. They have witnessed the promise of social media, but also how it has become perilously infected by monetization, greed, disinformation, and a loss of privacy.

My mother and father are very optimistic people, and they tend to look for the best in others. But history has taught them, and all of us, that human nature is not always wise and kind if left to its own devices.

We are presently attempting to integrate the power of humankind's collective scientific knowledge and innovation into an incredibly complicated and interconnected array of Earth ecosystems. These systems have evolved over a 4-billion-year span of time, almost all of which was without our presence. We must tread cautiously here.

We must use our remarkable advances to sustainably exist *within* Nature, and not vainly attempt to rule over it. Fighting Nature never works, especially in the long run.

If our new technologies are not carefully evaluated and regulated, many could represent existential threats to humankind. Once again, it is useful to recall the words of Albert Einstein when considering these risks:

"Intellectuals solve problems; geniuses prevent them."

With this notion firmly in mind, let's now examine a few emerging technologies.

Genetic Engineering

It is imperative that humankind collectively proceeds with research in genetic engineering (GE) – but to do so only with great caution, as we are manipulating the nucleotides of DNA, the very building blocks of Life itself.

Genetic engineering has been around for a few decades, but the techniques that were initially used to cut and splice genes were once quite blunt and non-exacting. That has all changed relatively recently with the advent of CRISPR technology – an acronym that stands for Clustered Regularly Interspaced Short Palindromic Repeats. In brief, this revolutionary process hijacks sophisticated technology from Nature (bacteria and viruses) to very precisely edit a living genome. Snip out an unwanted gene here, splice in a better gene there, and voila, you have a novel genetic sequence.

To date, the overall track record of genetic engineering has been quite poor in regards to agriculture, where it has arguably caused more problems than it has solved – although this could possibly change in the future.

As a general precept, when considering genetic manipulation, it is important to distinguish between *contained*-use vs. *non-contained*-use of GE (as described by scientists Michael Antoniou and John Fagan).

Genetic modification in agriculture is a *non*-contained-use method of GE, in that novel genetic variants are introduced into an open global ecosystem where they can reproduce and further mutate unchecked – which introduces a definite element of planetary risk.

As of yet, there have been no widely-utilized genetically engineered food crops that provide *inherently* increased yields, or that require significantly less water or fertilizer than traditionally-bred plants. Presently, GE plant yield increases are typically achieved via reduced competition with weeds and insects. However, pests can be managed with much more benign methods, such as using organic and integrated pest management (IPM) techniques. These methods are currently widely available, but they are less favored by many farmers because they are somewhat more expensive to employ (in the short-term).

The majority of presently utilized genetically modified crops have simply been bred to tolerate the application of herbicides (although some create their own insecticide); the result being a very large increase in the use of dangerous substances deposited on our food and in our environment. Farmers can now typically spray their entire field, including the GE crop and every square inch of soil, rather than pay more workers to pull or spray individual weeds.

Of note, any yield increase in currently utilized genetically engineered crops could likely be relatively short-lived – due to soil and ecosystem degradation, and the development of pesticide resistance.

This is not to say that genetically modified organisms (GMOs) in agriculture should be universally and forever condemned; rather that they should be further researched for possible future implementation, if less risky traditional breeding methods fall short.

Quite different from the above is *contained*-use genetic modification, where results have generally been quite good. For example, the genomes of certain bacteria have been modified, in isolation, to produce essential medications (such as insulin) for humans.

As mentioned, genetically modified bacteria could also soon play an important role in food production. Cultured microorganisms can be fed simple feedstock substrates in fermentation vats, using them to create complicated flavors, proteins, and other food substances.

Genetic modification of human *somatic* cells (via de-differentiation into stem cells and gene-editing) is presently being utilized to treat disease processes such as sickle cell anemia – and many other promising treatment possibilities are on the horizon.

More fraught with risk and moral hazard is the *non*-contained use of genetic engineering in human *germ* cells, wherein the DNA of human sperm or egg cells is edited, and new genetic traits therefore have the potential to propagate indefinitely in a family line.

This technology may be appropriate when used to remove a hereditable painful or deadly genetic trait; however, it is perhaps not always so wonderful when used to create a designer baby. The same technology that might allow parents to choose their child's eye-color, could also theoretically make it possible for rogue countries to create legions of super-warriors.

Many leaders in the field have sensibly recommended that the international genetic engineering community put the brakes on a bit, so that humankind can determine the best path forward in this endeavor.

Geoengineering

Presently, geoengineering most commonly refers to the large-scale human manipulation of planetary ecosystems to combat the effects of global warming.

There are various technological ways to intervene in Earth's climate systems, but one of the most controversial is to manage solar radiation by distributing tiny solar-reflecting particles into the stratosphere via airplanes – essentially crop-dusting the skies with sulfate aerosols that bounce sunrays back into space. This strategy attempts to somewhat imitate the planet-cooling effects created by large plumes of gas and ash emitted into the atmosphere from volcanic eruptions.

Proponents of deploying stratospheric sulfate aerosols point to the relative low cost and ease of lowering planetary temperatures via this method, believing that the possible sequelae of climate change may be so catastrophic that it is worth taking the risks that this process entails.

However, the risks associated with dispersed sun-blocking aerosols are indeed substantial. The long list of potential problems includes drought, decreased agricultural production, air pollution, acid rain, unequal global effects, loss of atmospheric ozone – and even possible climate warfare between nations.

Other solar radiation management ideas include marine cloud brightening (increasing the solar reflectivity of clouds by seeding them with plumes of seawater mist released from ships), space-based shading (launching disc-shaped lenses into orbit to deflect sunlight away from Earth), and increasing planetary surface reflectivity (such as using light-colored building materials in urban areas, or covering very large areas of sparsely inhabited land or sea with reflective material).

It is important to note that blocking or reflecting sunrays does not necessarily halt ocean acidification, which is currently happening due to excess oceanic absorption of carbon dioxide (CO_2). Attempting to *counteract* the greenhouse gas effects of CO_2 is not the same as *removing* it from the atmosphere – or, better yet, decreasing our emissions of it.

Continued production of CO_2 would further increase ocean acidity;

worsening the present deadly double-threat to coral creatures already imperiled by heat stress. With business as usual, most of these coral creatures – which have been absolutely essential to ocean ecosystems for millions of years –will likely not survive this century.

It is not sunrays that are causing rapid global warming, rather it is excessive CO_2 and other greenhouse gases that humans are producing that accentuate its effects. The Sun is the source of all life on our planet. We must keep our eye on the ball, focusing on the real cause of the problem – which is us. We need to stop creating so much CO_2.

Some scientists think that altering human habits will not be enough to keep global warming at a manageable level, and that we therefore need to find ways to actively *remove* carbon dioxide from the atmosphere.

Presently, technology-driven carbon dioxide removal (CDR) projects include:

1. *Using land-based carbon capture and storage* (CCS) methods at the point source of production (such as a coal-burning plant).

2. *Using direct air capture of carbon* (DAC) after it has been released into the environment (this process uses large fans to direct ambient air through a chemical filter to remove CO_2). At this time, future storage of captured carbon dioxide is planned to mostly be in large underground geologic repositories, such as depleted oil and gas fields, where leakage is a possibility.

3. *Using ocean-based carbon dioxide removal strategies.* Ideas here include raising seawater pH levels by altering its chemistry; fertilizing marine plankton so it will bloom wildly and absorb more CO_2; or artificially upwelling and downwelling seawater via pipes and pumps to increase plankton production, enhancing uptake of CO_2 via improved photosynthesis. However, these methods all suffer from scalability issues, and all come with very significant environmental risks.

At this point, technological carbon capture methods are still associated with very high costs, and they are thus not yet widely financially viable. Additionally, they utilize significant additional inputs of energy, and some land-based methods also require large amounts of water to function.

Of course, the simplest and least expensive way to remove carbon dioxide from the atmosphere is by returning Earth's forests to their natural composition and historic ranges via reforestation – letting trees do the work for us. And, restoring forest ecosystems to their native state provides numerous other important ecologic benefits as well.

Many geoengineering technologies truly have the potential to help manage the effects of climate change. However, they may also create unintended consequences – the so-called unknown unknowns.

There is also the potential moral hazard of legitimizing the techno-utopian belief that smart people and computers will solve all of our problems – which some individuals could use as justification for not altering personal behaviors. A sustainable future may indeed depend on technology, but it will depend equally on behavioral modification of the entire global populace.

Relatively small personal sacrifices must go hand-in-hand with scientific advances. Problems arise when citizens or companies are offered options that are easier than making real change – such as using carbon cap-and-trade schemes, or buying carbon-offset credits (e.g., individuals or companies can pay to have trees planted to help offset their emissions from air travel).

Some citizens and industries may not try as diligently to limit their carbon-emitting ways if they think there is a technological backstop to save them if things get out of control, or if they believe they have the option of buying their way out of the problem. Many people consider purchasing carbon offsets as similar to the eleventh century practice of buying indulgences from the church.

As there is no global governing body regarding geoengineering, some countries might choose to use options such as solar-blocking aerosols sooner rather than later. However, the risks of any type of climate manipulation have not been adequately studied, and these technologies are definitely not ready for primetime.

At least presently, many geoengineering ideas are considered by climate experts to be methods of last resort – believing that it is far easier to prevent problems now, than to figure out clever ways to fix them later.

Over four billion years in the making, our Earth is comprised of a majestic assembly of countless integrated systems of complexity, each exquisitely tuned to the others. History has shown that interrupting the balance of our planet's ecosystems has generally ended quite poorly. Like a mobile ceiling decoration hanging in a child's playroom, we cannot touch one part of it without moving the others.

We must act quickly regarding our climate crisis, as there are numerous environmental positive feedback loops that can each rapidly amplify the effects of planetary warming. In short, in regards to climate change, positive feedback loops generally mean that *the worse it gets, the worse it gets*. Here is an example:

One of the many positive feedback loops in climate science is the *albedo effect*, which is a measure of surface solar reflectivity. As highly *reflective* white Arctic Ocean ice melts, more highly *absorptive* dark sea water is exposed, warming the adjacent sea and air. This warmth causes even more ice to melt and more dark sea water to be exposed, which melts even more ice – feeding back on itself in an ominous upward spiral of increasing global temperature.

Again, this is but one of several worrisome positive feedback loops (with negative consequences) that are active today; all of whose effects on the climate are very difficult to accurately predict, as each one may potentiate the effects of the others.

As early manifestations of these feedback loops, we are presently witnessing troublesome changes in our Earth's atmospheric jet stream, and our oceanic Gulf Stream as well. We are experiencing resultant violent changes in weather patterns; such as hurricanes, flooding, and droughts that cause severe food insecurity and environmental destruction. Sea levels are also rising, which will result in massive societal displacement in coastal communities if we continue with business as usual.

Our Earth is also growing nearer to reaching ecologic *tipping points*, which are critical thresholds beyond which ecosystems may change very quickly, and possibly irreversibly. Tipping points could also increase the probability of triggering *other* tipping points, possibly resulting in a cascading domino effect.

The socio-economic effects of worsening climate change would be enormous, quite likely leading to global unrest, misery, and conflict.

The important thing to remember is that it really does not have to be this way. Humankind presently has the technology and resources available to rapidly change over to clean, sustainable, and renewable energy. We just do not yet collectively have the selflessness and resolve required to make minor sacrifices today, to avoid tremendous problems tomorrow.

If we continue to collectively abrogate our responsibility to preserve Earth's ecosystems for future generations, we may someday reach a point where technological climate manipulation is indeed needed. That would truly be a shame, because it would mean that we are amidst a global catastrophe that was once completely avoidable.

Personal actions that can help stop climate change:

We can each make some relatively minor lifestyle changes to decrease our carbon footprint. We can favor using electricity obtained from renewable sources like wind, water, and solar (rather than from natural gas or coal) to cook our food and heat our homes. We can keep our home thermostats at or below 66° F in winter (wear long underwear) and at or above 77° F in summer (wear shorts).

We can use air-travel less often, as the greenhouse gas effects of pollutants emitted high in the atmosphere are even worse than at ground level. Frequent air-travelers might try using video-conferencing for work when possible, and consider cutting back a bit on air-travel for vacations as well.

Hopefully, by the end of this decade, aircraft powered by hybrid battery/green hydrogen systems will be available for regional commercial travel ("green" hydrogen is obtained via electrolysis of water, using electricity obtained from a renewable energy source such as wind turbines or solar panels). Hybrid aircraft for long international trips will likely take somewhat longer to develop.

To further reduce transportation fuel usage, we can choose locally-produced food and consumer goods. We can consume less. We can drive a little more slowly to improve our gas mileage, which will lower emissions of greenhouse gases and other pollutants. We can consider changing over to an electric vehicle (EV) the next time we purchase a car or truck. EVs are not perfect, but they have fewer environmental downsides than internal combustion engines (ICEs). At least for now, EVs are the least dirty shirt in a pile of soiled laundry.

Finally, and perhaps most importantly, we can vote for leaders who champion a rapid global transition to clean and renewable energy; especially favoring wind, water, and solar-derived sources. Climate change absolutely represents an existential risk to all humanity – and this of course includes members of both the political left and right.

We should greatly appreciate the small number of people who make large sacrifices to radically decrease their carbon footprint. They are truly inspirational. But what we also need now are *massive* numbers of people each making relatively *small* sacrifices. This requires great governance and great messaging. We must choose leaders who possess a noble vision for a sustainable future – and the will to legislate change.

Artificial Intelligence, Robotics, and Virtual Reality

Artificial Intelligence (AI) and robotics have already greatly improved economic efficiencies in industry, and they have the potential to do far more. AI is also changing how we live; including the way we do our jobs, manage our finances, entertain ourselves, and stay healthy.

In medicine, AI is an emerging tool used to help radiologists evaluate chest CT scans – and it will likely soon be expanding into other forms of diagnostic imaging as well. AI will also help medical care providers analyze data to arrive at more accurate diagnoses, and subsequently create treatment algorithms custom-tailored to an individual's genome, lifestyle, and environment.

Robots presently assist in some surgeries, and there is more to come. Virtual or robotic caregivers are even starting to provide mental health care for patients in need.

Virtual reality (VR) will offer new entertainment and learning experiences for all – including the chance to virtually immerse oneself in new lands and cultures without the cost, energy requirements, or pollution associated with long-distance travel. VR also has very useful applications for training in medicine, engineering, and the military – and it will likely be used in numerous other fields as well.

AI and robotics will be used to efficiently perform many of the mundane chores of life; freeing up more time for intellectual pursuits, exercise, and recreational activities. Perhaps more of us will learn to play musical instruments, write novels and plays, and create beautiful pieces of art. Life could possibly be very wonderful – but only if AI, robotics, and virtual reality remain aligned with noble human interests.

AI enthusiasts like to talk about "singularity," which is the hypothetical inflection point at which AI becomes self-sufficient and advances beyond human intelligence. If singularity is ever realized, which is indeed quite possible, it will expose human civilization to several extremely dangerous challenges – a future of unknown unknowns, in an infinity of spinning coins of promise and peril.

And there is something else. Odd as it may sound, with technology comes the possibility that our lives could become *too* easy. If most of our work is performed by AI or robots, we humans could perhaps begin to lose our sense of relevance. As Sigmund Freud once said, love and work are "the cornerstones of our humanness."

We all need love, certainly. But we also need a reason to get up in the morning. We need purpose, meaning, and a sense of accomplishment. And we often get much of that from our work. We need to know that we matter; that we are relevant. The death of relevance portends the death of everything – sometimes even life itself.

A net loss of jobs (and perhaps relevance) to technology is just a possibility, not a prediction. People once worried that jobs would be lost by things like mechanized looms, and later by bank ATMs. There were job losses, certainly, but new jobs were also created.

There will indeed be some very painful transitions for many people, particularly middle-aged and older workers who are less likely to find replacement jobs, even if they get trained in a new career. The hope is that AI and robotics will *assist* us at the workplace rather than completely *replace* us – but the slope of "efficiency" could be slippery.

Another problem with AI is the loss of personal privacy. Someone or something will often be watching and listening. Sensors will be everywhere. They will be present on city streets – and at restaurants, grocery stores, and places of work, too. They will recognize our faces and our voices, and will have the ability to read our lips. They will even analyze our facial expressions to determine if we are happy, angry, or depressed. Merchants may attempt to use this information to target us with individualized ads. And governments may use this information to help maintain control of their citizens – for ill or good.

Virtual reality also has attendant risks, even when used for entertainment purposes. At its essence, the quest for a new reality could potentially imply that the world is not enough; that it is a place that must somehow always be enhanced or escaped from – using VR like a hallucinogen to withdraw from life or achieve a high. Like a drug, VR can be used to excessively expand or contract one's existence.

There is a degree of danger involved with continuously seeking something better, never accepting Life as it is, never being quite satisfied with our amazing existence on this fantastic planet, always searching for a version of happiness that is forever just out of reach.

Humanity evolved to flourish from *real* experiences with our Earth and its imperfect citizens. Perhaps we must fully immerse ourselves in "real" reality – creating as many new experiences with Nature and real humans as possible – before excessively venturing into the virtual.

Quantum Computing

Quantum computing is a relatively new technology that utilizes principles of quantum mechanics to massively increase computing power compared to other machines. In essence, currently used computers use binary technology expressed in bits, represented by a series of zeroes and ones; while quantum computers use qubits (quantum bits), which not only represent zeroes and ones, but also superpositions of states in between.

At the time of this writing, quantum computers are generally available only for large corporations and governments. That will likely change very soon – possibly within this decade.

Quantum computing offers tremendous potential in multiple areas, including assisting in the development of AI. It will use computer simulation rather than trial and error to create new medicines and materials, and will also improve forecasting of weather and climate change effects. As with many new technologies, quantum computing will also undoubtedly be used for many indications we have yet to imagine – the tech version of "If you build it, they will come."

However, as with many other technologies, with potential promise comes potential peril. Quantum computers may soon have the capability to break through encryption methods that keep the world's data safe – maybe even blockchain. That could be extraordinarily dangerous. Data regarding our personal financial information, our nation's power grids, and our military secrets and weapon-systems could all be vulnerable. It is a game of constant one-upmanship, where it is crucial to always stay one step ahead of the curve, creating safeguards today to protect against cyberthreats tomorrow.

Many governments and large corporations are working quickly to be the first-movers here. Quantum computing has the potential for a winner-take-all scenario, one in which there is the potential for tremendous power and financial gain. This power could be used to enhance the greater good – or it could be weaponized by malevolent global actors, intent on fomenting massive societal disruption.

Quantum computing and AI will certainly be used as critical elements of every nation's military arsenal. It is thus imperative that world leaders understand the existential threat this poses to humankind. It is vitally important that every world citizen realizes we are all in this together. Our fates will ultimately be the same – that of mutual gain, or that of mutual destruction. Constant communication is essential to keep that notion at the forefront of every mind.

Our new technology-infused reality is simultaneously exhilarating and terrifying, taking humanity on a breathtaking roller-coaster ride to a future that we can indeed help determine, if not yet precisely imagine.

It is already too late to ask ourselves if new technologies such as genetic engineering, AI, and quantum computing are really worth the risk. That train has left the station, and there is no backing up. Noble nations must lead and set the pace – while simultaneously working tirelessly at improving international diplomacy, and strengthening global institutions. Worldwide cooperation is vitally important, as we all live in each other's backyard. What affects one, affects all.

Forces of technology have truly saved the lives of people with cancer and other diseases. Yet these same forces have the potential to instantaneously take lives away; releasing demons of profound misery via the creation of massive disinformation, new viruses, and poisonous chemicals – and perhaps even the firing of nuclear missiles.

Have we opened Pandora's box? If so, maybe that first happened when our ancient ancestors created the first tools. In the end, will technology be worth it? Perhaps so. But humankind must remain ever-vigilant; using our sharpened blades only to create, and never to carelessly destroy. This will require great resolve and constraint – as well as unwavering international collaboration and regulation.

The journey to Sustainable Global Happiness will take a unified and comprehensive vision of a forever peaceful, just, and flourishing planet. It will take leaders with great courage and heart to help guide us. And, finally, it will take the combined determination of all Earth's citizens to make it happen – the will to achieve the global greater good.

TWELVE
The Greater Good

IT IS NOT easy to focus on others and the future when our genes and culture subconsciously nudge us toward self and immediacy. And it is fair enough to note that humans have advanced as far as we have by looking out for ourselves a bit, and having some fear of others and the unknown.

Nevertheless, it is essential to recognize that Life is constantly moving – and we must frequently adjust our sails to move with it. It is imperative that humankind continues to evolve; augmenting our subconscious predispositions with conscious rational thought.

It is quite easy to fall into the habit of reductionist thinking, as it is less mentally challenging to simply categorize people as either of light or dark skin color, rich or poor, progressive or conservative, etc. – often retreating to a primitive "us vs. them" tribalism.

As discussed earlier, human minds often make use of heuristics – mental shortcuts that rely on assumptions based on our past experiences. Without heuristics, we could easily become paralyzed with indecision, and something so simple as crossing a street could become a major endeavor. This type of fast reductionist thinking often works quite well at times when rapid decision-making is necessary, such as discerning if a dog running toward us is friendly or ferocious, and then quickly responding accordingly.

Humans often make snap judgments in emergency situations – but frequently at other times as well. As noted, the human mind often seems to want to take the easiest path, expending the least amount of energy. We thus often choose to see issues simply as black or white, rather than in more complicated shades of grey.

Of course, this rapid and easy type of thinking does not invariably work well, especially when evaluating chronic challenges that require more comprehensive thought.

The practice of reductionist labeling of other people may indeed offer an initially compelling cognitive shortcut. We can very simply decide that "conservatives" love capitalism, and "liberals" love socialism and the environment. Easy, right?

Not so fast. The problem, of course, is that the act of labeling is to paint with such broad strokes that no one truly understands what the labels stand for. We must be cautious of labels. If we name something, we often limit it; attempting to imprison a constantly-evolving entity into a single moment in time. Labels mean different things to different people at different times.

Recall that former President Richard Nixon, a Republican whom very few called "liberal," created the Environmental Protection Agency (EPA); signed the Marine Mammal Protection Act, the Endangered Species Act, and the Clean Air Act Extension – while also proposing the Safe Drinking Water Act.

If someone asks us whether we are "liberal" or "conservative," we can consider telling them that it depends on the issue; and that it also depends on their definition of those terms. We can tell them that we simply strive to always make the best decisions possible – decisions that provide the greatest good for the greatest number of people, while still trying to look out for the individual.

We can tell them the political left does not own the ideals of tolerance and equality, and the right does not own religion and the flag. We can tell them that it does not matter whether the ideals that we cherish are held by any particular political affiliation – because we are brave enough to cross party lines to achieve the greater good.

We can remind them there is great danger at both margins of the political spectrum. We can tell them that the continuum that includes liberal and conservative views is not best represented by a straight line – rather by a circle, with Passionate Centrism positioned at the top middle of the circle, where the greater good resides. The far edges, beyond center-left and center-right, begin to curve dangerously downward; ultimately converging together into radicalism, tyranny, and violence at a hellish common bottom.

We must not let violent outliers set policy or influence culture. The screams and shouts of outrageous individuals must be met and defeated with resolute calm and civil Passionate Centrism. Our very democracy is at stake.

It is important for a person to vote their conscience – but it must be with an *informed* conscience. Recall Juan Peron's observation that the masses do not think, the masses feel. We must be cautious to not validate this statement at our own individual level. Emotions are a necessary part of the human experience, certainly, but our emotions must be grounded in facts. Citizens do not have to choose between think *or* feel; rather we must choose to think *and* feel.

It is important to be aware of the biases of our information sources. We tend to hear a lot about the havoc created by outliers at the far-left and far-right, yet very little about the much quieter and more responsible middle. The truth is that there are far greater numbers of people who are center-left or center-right – they just don't make the news. Media networks know that good news generally does not ignite human emotions as strongly as bad news, and some seem willing to do whatever it takes to increase their viewership and advertising revenue.

If we listen to news sources at both ends of the political spectrum, we will quickly notice that they are each often filled with significant omissions and half-truths. Half-truths are often more dangerous than lies. A con-man often first gains trust by telling a truth.

Although much of what one hears or reads about in the news regarding an opposing party member may be true, reported statements and actions are often taken out of context or blown out of proportion – and similar admonitions of members of one's own side (perhaps well-deserved) are nowhere to be found. With many of our news sources, an unbiased *whole* truth is seldom offered.

Nevertheless, it is imperative to thoughtfully consider every person's point of view, even if it is far different than our own. There may be an element of truth to it. Ideals must evolve when necessary; especially if immutable facts indicate a better way to achieve the global greater good.

When choosing a potential leader of any nation, a candidate's personal integrity is immensely important – especially in times of crisis. If a citizen believes that a leader's character is somewhat irrelevant, as long as they advance their personal agenda, they are making a grievous error. If a leader cannot be trusted in small matters, they certainly cannot be trusted when billions of lives are on the line.

A noble vision for the future is an essential attribute of great leaders – and of everyday citizens as well. It is here that we each face a test of great consequence. Which vision will we choose? Will it be of a future that fearfully favors allegiances to self and tribe, seeking to divide and conquer perceived enemies? Or one that bravely unites Earth citizens together as friends, at home and abroad? We all decide how we wish to see the world – and we create our visions of the future from there.

If we choose to look for a world of darkness and enmity, we will indeed find it. And, if we choose to look for a world of light and love, that will surely be ours as well. Once again, we see what we look for.

PART IV

Good Captains and Good Maps

Navigating the Future

THIRTEEN
Noble Leadership and Foresight

FUTURE GENERATIONS WILL undoubtedly value many of the same things as we do today; such as clean air, pristine waters, verdant forests, rich soils, social justice, and a peaceful global populace – our guiding stars to a desirable future. It is not possible to plot an exact course to where humankind is going, but it is imperative that we never lose sight of these bright lights, each pointing the way to an ultimate destination of Sustainable Global Happiness.

Do not be disheartened by doomsayers; those who believe that humanity cannot, or will not, save itself. They are mistaken. We are not up against unconquerable forces. Two of our greatest foes are apathy and excessive self-interest – and each is defeatable via education and great messaging. We know our desired destination, we know how to prepare for the journey, and we know of the many challenges ahead.

Be aware, however, that reaching the grand destination of Sustainable Global Happiness is critically dependent on the actions of the captains of our ships – the leaders of our families, communities, and nations. It is also reliant on a charted plan of how to get there.

- In sum, we need good captains, and we need good maps.

The US and other nations must never retreat within their borders. Social injustice and environmental destruction happening in far-away places will impact our own lives at home. And not just today, but tomorrow as well. There is only one Earth; one planet where we all breathe each other's air and drink each other's water – and where we all live within reach of each other's bombs.

The challenges faced by our global brothers and sisters are our challenges as well. We are all in this together. Just as a good captain must weather every tempest with their crew, a noble leading nation must help all other nations overcome the trials and tribulations of the planet.

The journey to Sustainable Global Happiness will require momentous leadership, diplomacy, and international cooperation – as well as an advance of already established global governance and defense systems such as the United Nations and NATO. Some people may not like this idea, but there is no way around it. Most of the world's citizens don't want a nanny state; but it isn't that runny noses need wiped, rather it is that people need to be plucked out of the way of charging locomotives.

We cannot rely solely on the common sense and good graces of individual citizens, or even that of individual countries. That will not work well. Without an interconnected coalition of nations abiding by international laws and regulations, there would be chaos. If we rely on the hope that altruism and logical behavior will arise naturally from every corner of the Earth, we will soon be very disappointed – and living on a hot, polluted, and hostile planet.

It is vitally important for humankind to maintain a global network of international cooperation and good governance. This requires strong leadership. A noble and truly *united* America is essential to help lead the United Nations and other broad coalitions. Good governance not only summons the better angels of our nature; it also etches in stone a set of noble standards that all humankind can follow.

This is not to suggest that humankind should be controlled by one massive central world government. No, rather we can continue to foster a collaborative coalition of many diverse national governments; each independent, yet each working together toward the overarching ideal of Sustainable Global Happiness – i.e., *many* factions, *one* goal.

Today, some global citizens still favor a policy of isolationism. At first glance, this strategy may have a certain allure; but in practice it does not work well. Even if we were to ignore the many moral and environmental failings associated with an isolationist strategy, we cannot logically dismiss the fact that warring tyrants seldom respect national sovereignty. Every global border is vulnerable to this reality.

It is essential that the US remains proactively engaged with a broad network of allies; helping to *create* a future of our choosing, rather than letting the future happen to us.

We must strengthen all alliances that are designed to optimize the global greater good – especially the United Nations. Global unity is needed to effectively sanction rogue nations when necessary. We must also never distance ourselves from our NATO allies, or threaten their sovereignty. In addition, we must rejoin broad coalitions like the World Health Organization, and the other signatories of the Paris Climate Accord. We are stronger together.

We must not yield to our lesser selves, or to the apathy of the masses. Our nation must never give up on its extraordinary potential to achieve greatness – by coasting into mediocrity or descending into worse. We deserve better for ourselves. And the global children of the future certainly deserve better as well.

The US must help lead the way. If not us, who then? China? India? Presently, these nations are not yet demonstrating unwavering global leadership in regards to peace, social justice, and environmental sustainability. In many ways, the European Union (EU) is headed in the right direction; although it is very difficult to obtain consensus from 27 different member countries on every issue, and they cannot make a go of it alone. Even if other nations lead the way, they will certainly rely on US assistance to help overcome global challenges.

Some people may say that efforts at planetary peace and sustainability are futile, because other countries will continue to pollute the Earth and warm the climate; and aggressive nations are not likely to change their warring ways. But we cannot just keep pointing fingers at others. We are better than that. Leading nations rise up and lead, rather than descend into defensive postures of whataboutism.

Even with strong and noble US leadership, humankind could still possibly collectively fail to preserve our planet's peace, beauty, and bounty. But, if we act now, we still have a very good chance to achieve a positive outcome. In the absence of noble leadership, eventual societal and environmental planetary collapse is a near certainty.

It is true that China pollutes more than the US, but they also have a roughly four times higher population than ours. Per person, we emit significantly more greenhouse gases. And, importantly, one reason that China creates so much pollution is that the goods we use *here,* are often built *there.* A significant part of *their* pollution is due to *our* overconsumption.

Industries, and even governments, regularly encourage global citizens to consume more – because this of course increases corporate profits and government tax revenues. But it is imperative to maintain a panoramic perspective, keeping an eye on humankind's optimal destination of lasting global health and happiness. Chasing after short-term monetary gains at the expense of planetary sustainability is a fool's errand, portending an ultimate outcome of pain and misery.

Perhaps equally problematic is that our overconsumption has presently helped fill the financial coffers of global rivals, nations whose values are not always well-aligned with noble ideals of world peace and environmental sustainability. Countries flush with money are much less impacted by economic sanctions, thereby removing a vital geopolitical tool. Our obsession for more and more "low-cost" goods, if it continues, could possibly cost us dearly in the long run.

We presently see the effects of over-consumptive behavior regarding global interactions with Russia, even as it has invaded

Ukraine at the time of this writing. Many nations throughout the world are still importing massive amounts of Russian fossil fuels. And, even though Western countries have presently imposed economic sanctions on Russia, we have also carved out exceptions that allow some European nations to continue to buy Russian hydrocarbon fuels – an illogical step that adds to the war chest of a nation whose present actions are resulting in the deaths of children and other civilians.

We must stop this. Every citizen of every nation must make some minor personal sacrifices, resisting the temptation of buying "cheap" fossil fuels – which in reality come at a very high price. If we want to defeat a bully, we must be willing to take a punch.

Astonishingly, much of the world is still focused predominantly on carbon-based energy, even at a time when the UN Intergovernmental Panel on Climate Change (IPCC) has recently come out with a report stating that the climate crisis is even worse than we thought.

We thus have two existential reasons for every nation to be willing to endure the short-term financial pain associated with immediately shutting off *all* oil and natural gas spigots from *every* warring nation:

1. We can help deprive these regimes of the cash they need to fund their deadly war machines, and
2. We can help save our planet from environmental destruction.

It is time to make a heroic and globally-concerted effort, rapidly transitioning away from hydrocarbon consumption. We must quickly and massively add to our existing renewable energy infrastructure, especially with more wind turbines and solar panels.

To the naysayers, renewable energy options do indeed have some downsides – there truly is no free lunch. However, the potential societal and environmental perils of business-as-usual with oil and gas-based energy production are *far* greater than the risk of untoward events associated with a renewable energy future.

We must quickly and substantially increase the transmission cable connectivity of many varied sources of clean electricity between allied nations, which can then be shared amongst them. Depending on geographic location, as well as seasonal weather vagaries, nations with an abundance of one energy source, for instance hydropower, can trade with nations who may have an excess of solar or wind-derived energy available to them.

As a *short-term* emergency bridging mechanism, liquified natural gas (LNG) must continue to be widely exported as necessary to nations that have become dependent on acquiring hydrocarbon energy from unsavory global actors.

We must also be wary about making the same mistake twice, i.e., becoming dependent on foreign sources for our *clean and renewable* energy, just as we have been for our *carbon-based* energy.

Creating a renewable energy future requires critical minerals, most of which are presently mined and refined outside of the US (a very large percentage is sourced from China and other countries whose interests are not always well-aligned with ours). These critical minerals include neodymium used to build magnets for wind turbines and electric motors, tellurium and aluminum for solar panels, cobalt and lithium utilized in EVs; and many other elements as well.

The US is presently reliant on other nations for the materials crucial for building a society powered by clean and renewable energy. Any geopolitical disruption to global supply chains could represent a threat to US environmental, economic, and military security.

There are also humanitarian concerns in regards to obtaining these critical materials. Much of the cobalt used in batteries comes from the Democratic Republic of Congo, a significant portion of which is mined by thousands of children who would be much better off attending school. And, much of the polysilicon used in our solar panels is produced in the Xinjiang region of China, where there have been accusations of forced or coerced Uyghur labor.

We cannot continue to predominantly follow a "low-cost" model regarding our energy economy; rather we must make the long-term investment necessary to develop critical mineral production at home and in allied countries.

We must also be careful to not put all our energy eggs in one basket – such as assuming that lithium batteries will always be the most efficient and sustainable power source for EV transportation and energy storage. The tremendous potential for a future "green" hydrogen energy economy must be recognized and advanced as well.

One hundred years from now, it is quite possible that solar panels and wind turbines could be yesterday's news, perhaps replaced by other energy-producing sources – such as nuclear fusion.

Currently-utilized nuclear *fission* reactors create energy by *splitting* atoms, whereas *fusion* reactors may someday commercially create energy by *joining* atoms together. Although fusion reactions do indeed create some radioactive waste, the half-lives of the products they produce are markedly shorter than those created by nuclear fission reactions. The creation of long-lived radioactive products, with no place to store them safely and inexpensively, is one of many serious drawbacks associated with deriving energy from nuclear fission.

It is certainly important to fund research for moonshot projects like fusion. However, it is also imperative to not divert too many resources away from today's proven energy technologies already provided by our Sun – which is the ultimate fusion reactor.

Energy from our Sun's rays are of course easily captured by photovoltaic solar panels. Our Sun also heats the Earth unevenly, which creates wind that can be harnessed by wind turbines to produce electricity. This wind also blows clouds over land masses, where rainwater is dropped, forming rivers which can be used to create hydroelectric energy. We *already* have a great solution to our energy problem, which is to fully utilize the power of our own fantastic star.

Humankind can presently safely create all of the energy we need by carefully utilizing our renewable wind, water, and solar sources of power. These energy sources – and the storage technologies to support them – must continue to evolve. It is critical that we relentlessly fund energy research; finding less expensive and more ubiquitous alternatives for many of the critical minerals and systems presently employed to deliver clean and sustainable energy to all.

It is imperative that international leaders come together to stop individual citizens, corporations, and nations from degrading the environment and abusing human rights. Words of condemnation and concern are not enough. It is time for resolute action against complicit complacency and greed, which always work against environmental sustainability and social justice.

Resolute action means enforcing strict environmental and human rights regulations – using fines, criminal charges, and massive economic sanctions when necessary. Resolute action means we must each be willing to accept a small amount of personal sacrifice to achieve the global greater good.

Without US leadership, or at least its substantial cooperation, there is little hope for the global citizens of the future. Knee deep in water, all could perish on the same sinking ship, gaining little solace from placing blame on each other's ancestors. The US must help lead.

And the US must become a *selfless* global leader. Today, numerous countries are in upheaval, and the world needs a role model. Strongmen are popping up everywhere. Nativism and populism are exploding. The US cannot set a "me first" example, and then expect that others will not follow suit.

The United States must balance its examples of power with the power of its example. The most successful leaders rely on inspiration, selflessness – and great diplomacy.

Communication and Compromise

In 1987, US President Ronald Reagan and Soviet General Secretary Mikail Gorbachev signed a historic arms control agreement banning the use of intermediate-range nuclear missiles.

These leaders were able to overcome 40 years of Cold War ideology, and they did so by frequently communicating, collaborating, and compromising with each other. As a result of numerous letters written between them, as well as four major summit meetings, the relationship between the two leaders transformed from one of adversaries into one characterized by a much more friendly rivalry.

Recurrent face-to-face meetings between world leaders in their respective homelands is critically important. As the saying goes, "The best way to get rid of an enemy is to make them your friend." Friends don't bomb each other.

Of course, some of our adversaries today are not likely to abruptly change their ways and immediately start interacting well with others. There is often no reasoning with a sinister madman or ideologue. Nevertheless, even if attempts at diplomacy are not initially fruitful, in most cases it is imperative to maintain frequent communication with both friend and foe alike. As another saying goes, "Keep your friends close, and your enemies closer."

We are perhaps not likely to significantly alter many other global leaders' plans for world economic leadership – just as they are not likely to change ours. However, some of these other leaders are willing to use massive cyber-attacks – as well as invade and plunder – to achieve their country's financial and ideological goals.

The US and other nations must utilize every means possible to avoid such catastrophes, including relentless attempts at diplomacy. If diplomatic measures are unsuccessful, we will nevertheless have the momentum of favorable public opinion on our side – which is a very formidable force indeed. Global citizens are much more willing to rally for a noble cause than for a malevolent leader.

Reagan and Gorbachev found common ground because they had a joint desire to diminish an existential threat, that of global nuclear annihilation. Today, we still face this same existential threat – as well as possibly many more created by the advent of new technologies and a growing global populace.

With continuous dialogue and recurrent diplomatic missions, the US and other nations can collaborate with competitors to achieve the global greater good. We have done it before.

A new world order is forming, and it will likely be politically, economically, and militarily dominated by an assembly of several different nations – some whose philosophies and values have not historically been well-aligned with our own. Nevertheless, we must continuously engage in pointed discussions; attentively listening to the concerns of our rivals, while always offering our point of view as well.

We must also remember that actions speak louder than words. We must *show* global citizens that we seek a peaceful, just, and flourishing Earth. We must *show* leaders of other nations that democracy works, and that fostering religious freedom creates a peaceful populace.

And, crucially, we must *show* the world that the citizens and states of the US are indeed united, and that our coalitions with allied nations are united as well.

United We Stand

Our country must relentlessly strive for internal unity. US citizens have come together many times previously – and not just in times of war. About fifty years ago, NASA's Apollo spaceship project brought together a multitude of individuals and businesses in an audacious plan to land a person on the Moon.

This incredible accomplishment was made possible by a collection of over 400,000 US workers – and thousands of industrial companies and universities – all working together as a unified team. Most of these dedicated individuals cared little about the political leanings of their fellow workers, choosing instead to focus intently on a worthy common goal. We must follow their lead today.

The US must wisely choose the economic sectors we wish to advance. The practice of arming potentially dangerous regimes with advanced weapons built here at home is a dangerous venture. In the last two decades, about one-third of our weapons sales went to countries that were not our allies. Tenuous relationships built on money can easily erode; and we could someday be attacked by the very fighter planes we ourselves built. There are much better ways to bankroll a nation – especially as we now have a window of opportunity to become a vanguard of a massive global renewable energy economy.

The US can find both happiness and financial security by directing our efforts toward an economy powered by clean and renewable energy (especially wind and solar). This will help ensure a sustainable planet – as well as serve as a tremendous driver of job growth, economic prosperity, and even national pride and unity. It will also cut off funds to aggressive and emboldened rogue nations, who have grown rich by selling their petroleum and natural gas products to a world that should have known better.

Clean and renewable energy is not only critically necessary for environmental sustainability, it is also crucially important for global financial stability, as well as for international peace and security. Leaders on both sides of the aisle must all come together, pushing quickly for an economy powered by clean and renewable energy.

Civic Virtue

There are many technology visionaries who believe we must capitalize on human ingenuity to solve our problems. They are correct. Novel ideas and innovation will indeed be necessary. However, relying solely on new technologies to solve all our problems neglects the obvious. We will need technology, certainly. But we will equally require civic virtue, willpower, and good governance.

When planning humankind's future, it is of course important to look at the short term; making plans for the days, weeks, months, and coming year ahead. However, it is also imperative to look further; creating goals for each decade to come, and for the rest of this century as well.

And we should not stop there. Honoring the idea of intergenerational equity, humankind can extend its vision even more, to include at least the entirety of this millennium – which is still just a blink of the eye in geologic time.

The foundation of foresight and action built by the framers of the US Constitution nearly 250 years ago still helps support global citizens today. It is now our turn to do the right thing. What will **we** do to benefit future global citizens? What will **our** noble legacy be?

A central premise of these pages is that the individual, the collective, and the Earth itself – Person, People, and Planet – are inseparably connected, in time and in space. What affects one today, affects all tomorrow; locally and abroad. It is imperative that citizens of all nations fully embrace this idea.

In the US and many other countries, we still have the opportunity to vote honorable and courageous leaders into office. If we are not careful, that luxury might not last. We must always honor the voting process. We must vote for leaders of good character; men and women who possess a long-term vision of a safe, just, and flourishing planet comprised of sustainable ecosystems and peaceful citizens.

We must not vote with our personal pocketbook foremost in our minds; rather we must vote for the global greater good – the good of our country and the good of all world citizens, present and future. Noble actions directed toward others will eventually come full circle, touching our own lives, improving our own personal well-being.

Each of us must play our individual role in a grand communal effort to achieve Sustainable Global Happiness. In the end, leaders of nations and neighborhoods are made up of people like you and me.

Let's each do our part.

FOURTEEN

A Map to Sustainable Global Happiness

A COMPREHENSIVE PLAN for the future must acknowledge that one's personal health and happiness are inseparably connected to the health and happiness of the Earth and *all* its inhabitants. We are all in this together – what affects one, affects all. It takes a healthy planet – with rich soils, fresh air, clean water, and happy fellow citizens – to make a fully healthy and happy human.

This plan for the future must consider that the sustainable carrying capacity of our planet may presently be less than 5 billion people (the current global population is now 8 billion). It must take into account the predicted net *negative* effect on world food production and human health from rising global temperatures and environmental toxins. It must address the enormous task of changing global behavior patterns of overconsumption – which are getting worse instead of better. And it must also acknowledge that without a peaceful and sustainable planet of abundance, nothing else is possible.

A proposed action plan is presented below, using the acronym PEACEFOOD. This plan focuses on the base layers of Maslow's Hierarchy of Needs, emphasizing meeting basic human safety and physiologic requirements – Peace and Food – in a sustainable fashion. The universal availability of healthy food, clean air, and pure water are vital elements of a peaceful planet.

The first letter of PEACEFOOD stands for **P**opulation, as it is an essential step to stabilize human population numbers via improved education and access to affordable contraception. If the foundation of humanity's Happiness is a flourishing Earth, the cornerstone is a sustainable population. Overpopulation intensifies nearly every challenge that our planet and its inhabitants face.

The last letter of the acronym stands for **D**emocracy and **D**iplomacy, as each of these ideals are critical foundations of a flourishing Earth community.

On the following pages a proposed map to Sustainable Global Happiness is presented – an evolving action plan that offers global guideposts as starting points for collaborative discussion.

PEACEFOOD
Population- **E**nergy- **A**griculture- **C**limate- **E**ducation- **F**orests- **O**ceans- **O**pen spaces- **D**emocracy/Diplomacy

Population: Aspirational goal of a global fertility rate of 2.0 or less, leading to a steady-state Earth population of approximately 5 billion (down from 8 billion presently).

Energy: The long-term ultimate aspirational goal is a zero-carbon economy. Wind/Water/Solar/Geothermal energy technologies to replace coal, natural gas, and nuclear energy.

-Ban the sale of new internal combustion engine (ICE) cars/trucks by 2030 (note: in 2025, 96% of all new car sales in Norway were EVs). Raise gas/diesel tax by $1/gal. to help offset the social cost of carbon.[1]

-Massively increase clean public transportation options via electric and/or hydrogen powered buses and electric high-speed trains.

-Tighten energy efficiency standards for commercial buildings and homes. Set thermostats at 66° F (19° C) or lower in winter and 77° F (25° C) or higher in summer.

Agriculture: Regenerate and sustain land, water, and air for present and future generations. Global aspirational goals include:

-Move toward an *organic* agriculture model. Use fewer:

> *Synthetic insecticides*. 50% reduction by 2030, and eventual ban. Employ Integrated Pest Management (IPM) techniques, and further develop biologic insect control methods.
>
> *Synthetic herbicides*. 50% reduction by 2030, and ban by 2035. Control weeds by human-power, machines, robots, cover crops, and polyculture plantings.
>
> *Synthetic fertilizers*. 25% reduction by 2030; 50% by 2040. Precision Agriculture and Agroecology techniques improve nitrogen use efficiency (currently 55% globally and 70% in US).

-Fertile cropland must not be *primarily* dedicated to raising food for animals. Cows, sheep, and goats to be grass-fed and grass-finished on pastureland, closely simulating wild herbivore feeding and movement patterns (i.e., holistic ranching). Grazing cover crops and post-harvest material by livestock as a *secondary* project is encouraged. All farm animals to be treated humanely and given daily access to outdoor living space. No cropland to be *primarily* used for biofuel.

-Set aside areas of biodiverse green space on all farms. No ground left uncovered by plant life. Cover crops to be used in all fields, which are preferably mowed or roller-crimped rather than tilled.[2]

-Embark on a global campaign to reduce food waste 25% by 2030, and 50% by 2035.

-Reduce consumption of meat and other animal products. Animal protein to be partly replaced by protein from tree nuts and legumes; and possibly by alternative meat products, marine microalgae supplemented foods, and Precision Fermentation. Meat consumption quantity to be influenced by global population numbers, climate change factors, new food technologies, and market forces.

Climate: Achieve Net Zero carbon by 2035 – as recently pledged by Finland (the US goal is presently 2050). Net Zero to be reached via marked *reduction* of carbon emissions, and augmented by carbon *removal* via massive reforestation (and possibly by mechanical carbon capture and storage if needed as an emergency bridging strategy).

-Markedly reduce greenhouse gas (GHG) emissions: Address *the CO_2 problem* by choosing sustainable (wind/hydro/solar) energy and electric vehicle transportation; *the methane problem* by eating less beef, and discontinuing fracking for natural gas; and *the nitrous oxide problem* by significantly decreasing synthetic nitrogen fertilizer use. Phase out *hydrofluorocarbon* refrigerants.[3]

-Phase out cap-and-trade and carbon offset schemes (each work too slowly and not well enough; and carbon offsets disproportionately affect indigenous populations and frontline communities).

-Provide massive financial *incentives* (e.g., rebates, tax credits, loans) for renewable energy production; and concurrently *penalize* excessive GHG emission offenders with progressively increasing fines – i.e., use dual reward and punishment systems. Stop all oil and gas subsidies.

-Consider conservation payment strategies for sustainable land conversion and restoration efforts.

Education: Help provide education for all children globally. Include lessons on local and global civic virtue – as well as on population awareness, social justice, environmental sustainability, liberal arts, and science/technology/engineering/math (STEM).

Forests: Halt deforestation. No new trees planted for biofuel use. Sustainable, non-clear-cut harvest from existing managed forests to provide lumber is allowed, with a diverse polyculture replanting after harvest. Massively step-up efforts at reforestation and afforestation.

Oceans: Legislate sustainable harvest management. Place a moratorium on fishing for threatened species. Fishing subsidies phased out by 2030. Preserve and rehabilitate coastal estuaries and wetlands. Reduce/reuse/recycle plastic, which is a major source of ocean pollution. *Reduce* is most important. Immediately spearhead a reconvened UN Convention of the Seas, with modified regulations to reflect current concerns.

Open spaces: Encourage biodiversity by rewilding land. Protect and expand wild areas; provide corridors between these core areas; and reintroduce/protect all keystone species living in them. Consider biologist E.O. Wilson's "Half-Earth" strategy as an aspirational goal, in step with a decrease in human global population numbers.

Democracy/Diplomacy: Champion freedom and equality for all Earth citizens.

A) Strengthen democracy: Mandate *term limits, ranked choice voting, electoral college voting reform, campaign finance reform, and competency testing for federal government leaders*. Maintain *constitutional separation of powers*.

- Term limits: In the US, term limits could be set at two 2-year terms for Congress House members; one 6-year term for Senate members; and one 8-year term for Supreme Court Justices.
- Ranked-choice voting: The odds of electing ideologically extreme lawmakers are lowered with this system.[4]
- Electoral College voting reform: Although the elimination of the Electoral College is favored by the majority of US citizens, this requires a Constitutional amendment, which is presently unlikely to be politically tenable. A possibly more viable option is The National Popular Vote Interstate Compact (NPV), a state bill requiring that all of a state's electoral votes go to the winner of the *national* popular vote, rather than the winner of the *state* popular vote.
- Campaign finance law reform. Repeal the US Supreme Court 2010 *Citizens United* decision. This ruling currently allows wealthy donors to greatly influence the political system by spending unlimited amounts of money on elections.
- Competency testing: Require testing of *all* political candidates (regardless of age) who seek elected federal office in Congress or the office of the President. Testing would also be required of all potential Cabinet members and Supreme Court Justices, prior to nomination for Senate confirmation. Competency testing would assess critical thinking skills, and fund of knowledge regarding history, current geopolitics, and economics.

-<u>Separation of powers</u>: Faithfully maintain the jurisdictional authority – and checks and balances – of our co-equal executive, legislative, and judicial branches of government.

B) *<u>Strengthen diplomacy</u>*:
-Continue ongoing efforts to communicate and compromise with all citizens, at home and abroad. Champion the ideal of a truly *united* USA, helping to lead a strong United Nations.
-Foster ongoing international discussions regarding:
    -Ensuring religious freedoms.
    -Providing a living wage for all full-time workers.
    -Providing basic health care for all.
-Acknowledge the shared existential threat that nuclear weapons and other forms of warfare pose to the entire global populace. Maintain and honor a strong military to defend homeland and allies, but commit to a policy of "no first strike" action with nuclear weapons. Engage military personnel internationally only as part of a contingent of allies called to defend the lives of endangered global citizens. Seek peace!

PEACEFOOD Notes:

1. US Federal gas/diesel tax (now 18.4 cents/gal and 24.4 cents/gal) would be immediately raised by $1/gal (avg $523 per car per year), to help offset the social cost of carbon (avg $851 per car per year). Figures are based on average US passenger vehicle emissions of 4.6 metric tons of CO_2/year, 11,500 miles driven/year, 22 mpg fuel efficiency, and a 2022 *Nature* journal article estimated mean social cost of carbon of $185/metric ton (note: 2023 EPA estimate is $190/metric ton). Other nations could similarly raise fuel taxes, as applicable.
2. Tillage causes erosion, run-off of nutrients, evaporation of water, destruction of healthy soil organisms, and increased CO_2 emissions. Cover crops increase soil fertility, absorb atmospheric CO_2, and naturally control weed growth.
3. Hydrofluorocarbon (HFC) refrigerants replaced ozone-depleting CFCs banned by the Montreal Protocol in 1987. However, even though HFCs do not deplete the ozone layer, they do have very potent greenhouse gas effects.
4. With ranked-choice voting, voters rank all candidates in preferential order. The candidate with the least number of votes is eliminated, and the second choice of any person who voted for this candidate is awarded to the voter's second-choice candidate. The process continues until one candidate wins by reaching more than a 50% majority. With this system, votes for "third-party" candidates unlikely to win are no longer potentially "wasted" votes, because every vote still counts.

Guideposts to Personal Happiness to Consider:

1. **Believe.** Believe in something greater than ourselves – a greater Presence or purpose characterized by forgiveness, peace, and love. Lean in to hope; if even just a hope in great possibilities.
2. **Give.** Love our neighbors as ourselves – sharing our riches with other Earth citizens, at home and across the globe. Acknowledge their struggles; attend to their needs. Love deeply, love broadly.
3. **Cherish our Earth.** Protect it. Reduce/reuse/recycle. Consume less; favoring a life of lean abundance. Avoid adding chemicals to our land, water, and air. Immerse in Nature, enjoying our planet's fantastically diverse ecosystems and creatures. Observe a flower up close, noting both its simple beauty and exquisite intricacies.
4. **Eat Right.** Favor locally produced, organic, whole foods – about half of which are vegetables and fruits. Eat in a 10-hour or less window of time, and stop eating 4 hours before bedtime. Limit sodium intake and added sugar. Avoid preservatives, unnatural dyes, and other food additives. Read the label on all foods consumed.
5. **Drink Right.** Choose clean filtered water for the majority of fluid intake. Try not to drink anything out of a can or bottle (aim for never more than once per week) – and never out of plastic.
6. **Sleep Right.** Bedtime is a sanctuary for rest. Banish any troubles to another place. Aim for about 8 hours of sleep each night. Follow a regular sleep routine. Keep bedrooms cool and dark, but allow morning sunlight to come in. Be outside for at least 30 minutes of sunlight each day. Enjoy a period of quiet relaxation before bedtime.
7. **Exercise.** Aim for at least 30 minutes per day. Always make time for this. Mix up our activities. Keep moving. Have fun with it!
8. **Meditative Stretching.** Set aside time for quiet solitude each day. Combine gentle stretching and movement with meditation. Consider adding some relaxing music in the background.
9. **Smile.** Find something uplifting to laugh or smile about every day – if even for just a moment in times of challenge. Look for the good.
10. **Engage.** Connect with as many people as possible. Talk with a friend or family member each day – and always let them know how much we love them.
11. **Forgive.** Forgive others and ourselves. No person is perfect.
12. **Be positive.** Positive thoughts and words lead to positive actions. Imagine a world of great Happiness – for ourselves, and all present and future inhabitants of a flourishing Earth…Make it happen.

Epilogue

THOSE OF US living in the United States and other rich countries generally spend most of our lives warm, safe, and dry. We usually eat until we are full, often enjoying meals more lavish than a king's banquet of yesteryear. We have the opportunity to travel to fantastic cities, visit magnificent forests, and walk alongside beautiful lakes, streams, and oceans. We have a wonderful array of sports and games to play and watch. We have countless books, movies, and music options to entertain us. Yet we often still want more.

We are not typically confined to a hospital bed, where someone must help us with a bedpan, or administer medications to us each day. We have the opportunity to ride a bicycle like a kid again if we wish; or go for a swim in a lake on a hot summer day. We can slide or ski or board down a mountain of pure white powder snow; or run on a trail through a meadow of wildflowers – just for the pure joy of it. Yet we often still want more.

We often have a friend to sit with by an evening fire. We may even have a life companion to embrace under the light of a rising full moon. At days end we can rest, looking up at a night-sky full of wonder. Before drifting off to sleep, we can call our children or other loved ones to wish them goodnight, or even give them a hug if they live nearby. Only very few of us have a friend or family member engaged in battle, whose very life we must pray for each night. Yet we often still want more…

We must decide to focus on what we have, not on what we don't have. We can choose to live a life of wonder and awe over the absolute magnificence of our planet; grateful for the opportunity to be such an integral part of the majesty of our universe.

We can laugh and smile every chance we get. We can forgive ourselves and others. We can love deeply, and love broadly. We can look for light – and we will find it.

One hundred years from now, no one will care how much money we made, what we did for a living, or what kind of clothes we wore. But maybe, just maybe, some child of the future will be a little happier because of something we did.

Maybe a child of the future will rest in the shade of a tree that we planted. Or maybe they will smile after reading a poem that we wrote. Maybe they will become a wonderful musician, because we taught their great-great grandparent how to play a musical instrument, and each of their subsequent family generations taught the next.

Maybe a child of the future will look out over rolling green hills, enjoying an heirloom apple they picked from a nearby field, because one hundred years earlier we supported an orchardist there by purchasing their slightly more expensive organic produce.

Maybe a child of the future will swim alongside magnificent ocean fishes and bright-colored coral; because we chose to tread lightly on our planet – minimizing our personal footprint by consuming less, and choosing clean and renewable sources for our energy.

Maybe all children of Earth will have friends of every size and shape and color and religion, and never once give this a second thought; because we once showed their ancestors how to look for similarities and goodness in people, and the example we set was passed along.

We can close our eyes and create a vision of future Earth residents in our mind; right now, if we wish. Look closely, and we can see them beyond each turn – happy citizens of the future, forever playing and working together on a safe, just, and beautiful Earth.

Acknowledgments

I am grateful for my family members and friends, many of whom were early readers of various iterations of the manuscript. Your insights, questions, counterpoints, and words of encouragement have helped make this a better book. We of course do not always agree on every subject, but we share the common goal of optimizing the global greater good.

This book is a composite of the thoughts, words, and actions of the many people who have helped shape my life – the multitude of diverse artists whose creative works add such beauty and joy to living; the authors of the many books, essays, and studies I have read; the teachers, colleagues, and mentors who have personally influenced my way of thinking; and the numerous family members and friends who have enriched me with their love.

My life is the attempted creative synthesis of what I admire most about each of you – even though I often fall short of my aspirations to follow in your footsteps. The words on these pages are drawn from a wellspring of knowledge, love, hope, tears, and laughter you have shared with me.

My heartfelt thanks to all.

"We shall find peace. We shall hear angels. We shall see the sky sparkling with diamonds."

-Anton Chekhov

Randy A. Siltanen, MD has worked as a physician in Primary Care Medicine, and then later in Diagnostic Imaging. He now writes about creating personal and collective happiness on a just and flourishing Earth. He is the author of *In the Midst of Paradise*.

Randy resides in the western United States with his wife Diana.

www.ingramcontent.com/pod-product-compliance
Lightning Source LLC
Chambersburg PA
CBHW031643040426
42453CB00006B/199